Anonymous

Talks with Athenian Youths

Translations from the Charmides, Lysis, Laches, Euthydemus, and Theaetetus of

Plato

Anonymous

Talks with Athenian Youths
Translations from the Charmides, Lysis, Laches, Euthydemus, and Theaetetus of Plato

ISBN/EAN: 9783337189419

Printed in Europe, USA, Canada, Australia, Japan

Cover: Foto ©ninafisch / pixelio.de

More available books at **www.hansebooks.com**

WITH ATHENIAN YOUTHS

TRANSLATIONS

FROM THE

CHARMIDES, LYSIS, LACHES, EUTHYDEMUS,
AND THEAETETUS

OF

PLATO

—

NEW YORK
CHARLES SCRIBNER'S SONS
1891

PREFACE.

Xenophon tells us that Socrates always went where he could meet most people; that in workshop and market-place, at the festive board or in the palaestra, he conversed with all men alike, whatever their class or profession. But while no opportunity was neglected of mingling with and, as it were, feeling the heart of his fellow-citizens, the companions most truly congenial to him were not men of his own age, but a later generation, — the youth of Athens. This, at all events, is what we gather from our chief source of information concerning Socrates, the works of Plato. In nearly all the so-called dramatic dialogues, where not only Socrates the thinker but Socrates the man is revealed to us, it is these charming youths who lend life and animation to the scene and who inspire the master's noblest utterances. And indeed these fresh young minds, filled with eager questionings and unsatisfied longings, may well have called forth the best powers of one whose mission it was to turn the eye of the soul towards the Truth.[1] For to Socrates education meant not crowding the mind with "knowledge from without," allowing no room for the play of independent thought or the growth of individual character, but the building up of character by the charm of good words[2] and by examples of high thoughts and noble lives,[3] and the awakening to life and activity of that intuitive knowledge of realities which, as he believed, exists in every human soul.

[1] *Republic*, 519 B.   [2] *Charmides*, 157 A.   [3] *Laches*, 180 C.

Perhaps nowhere more clearly than in the dialogues before us do we see the attitude of Socrates towards his younger followers, or rather his fellow-searchers for truth, — for as such he preferred to regard them. If a touch of his accustomed irony may be discerned in a somewhat exaggerated self-depreciation and deference to their opinions, we mark at the same time his encouragement of their efforts, his ready adaptation to their limited powers of understanding, and above all his steady determination that they shall use their own faculties, and always say what they think.[1]

The application of this apparently simple rule was fraught with peculiar difficulties in a period of transition such as that in which the mission of Socrates was begun. Old schools of philosophy had lost their power and vitality, while the new conceptions destined to lay the foundations of modern philosophy were as yet in process of evolution. Meanwhile the field temporarily left vacant was occupied by eristics, or masters " in the art of word-fighting."[2] Then indeed with truth might men be called " slaves of their words."[3] It needed only that a proposition should be boldly enunciated by some "teacher of wisdom," for it to become straightway an axiom; and the more unintelligible was its meaning, apparently the more readily was it adopted. For logic, as yet an unknown study, had not taught men to see through verbal fallacies and consider each proposition in its exact meaning, not "tricked out with empty words."[4] Failing to distinguish between forms of thought and forms of expression, they regarded the two as identical and interchangeable, while their unfamiliarity with abstract ideas constantly led them to confuse the abstract with the concrete.

---

[1] *Theaetetus*, 171 D.   [2] *Euthydemus*, 272 A.
[3] *Theaetetus*, 173 C.   [4] *Laches*, 196 B.

The urgency with which Socrates insisted upon a clear-cut definition of every term as a necessary preliminary to any discussion marks a new era in thought. The effort, however unsuccessful, to define any abstract idea or quality must of necessity throw some light upon its essential nature, even when nothing is effected beyond eliminating false conceptions of it. Subjected to this test, the stock sayings which had formerly passed unchallenged were proved unmeaning and worthless, and he who had most loudly proclaimed them was, "as if by a torpedo fish," torpified into silence.[1] Nor is this all. Not content with having convicted him of pretending to know when he really knows nothing,[2] Socrates follows up his victim until he has compelled him to strip and try himself against him in argument,[3] and has finally extorted from him an account of how he is "now living and has lived in the past."[4] Nor is it from ill will that he thus deprives men of the false conceptions endeared by long familiarity, but because he is constrained by the law of his nature "never to consent to a lie or to stifle the truth."[5]

A process which has for its chief object the clearing away of old misconceptions and prejudices by what Grote calls the "negative arm of philosophy, without which the positive arm will but strike at random,"[6] is not likely to commend itself to those whose minds, deep set in the grooves of custom and tradition, are conscious of no defect in the old loose methods of thought. Instances, to be sure, are not wanting of older men who, like Nicias, deem it no evil thing to be called to account for whatever they have done or are now doing that is not right;[7] but in the main it is the young

---

[1] *Meno*, 80 A.
[2] *Apology*, 23 D.
[3] *Theaetetus*, 169 B.
[4] *Laches*, 187 E.
[5] *Theaetetus*, 151 D.
[6] Grote's *Plato*, vol. i. p. 388.
[7] *Laches*, 188 A.

who, untrammelled by the bonds of pride or self-interest, and "capable of progress in everything,"[1] willingly lend themselves to the healing cross-examination, and are finally enabled to "bring out more than was within them"; to "discover of themselves many noble truths."[2]

Had it been the original intention of Plato to arrive at any definite and satisfactory conclusion in these particular dialogues, he must certainly have acknowledged his own failure. The definition of temperance which is attempted in the *Charmides*, that of friendship in the *Lysis*, and that of courage in the *Laches*, are finally confessed to be altogether inadequate, while the examination of the practical value of philosophy undertaken in the *Euthydemus*, and that of the true nature of knowledge in the *Theaetetus*, are at last abandoned as hopeless. "The lights which Plato throws upon his subject," Jowett observes, "are indirect; but," he continues, "they are not the less real for that. He has no intention of proving a thesis by a cut-and-dried argument; nor does he imagine that a great philosophical problem can be tied up within the limits of a definition. If he has analyzed a proposition or notion, even with the severity of an impossible logic, if half-truths have been compared by him with other half-truths, if he has cleared up or advanced popular ideas or illustrated a new method, the aim of a Platonic dialogue has been attained."[3]

It is nevertheless undeniable that there is much in Plato's writings which is not only inconclusive but well-nigh incomprehensible to readers not familiar with the state of knowledge at that time. Our intellectual status is so different from that of the Greek world of the fourth century before Christ, that questions then deemed worthy of careful

---

[1] *Theaetetus*, 146 B.   [2] *Ibid.* 150 D.
[3] Jowett's Introduction to *Theaetetus*.

elucidation now seem to us childish and trivial, while points which we should deem of vital necessity to the discussion are not once mentioned, doubtless because they were not even perceived. The modern reader, moreover, who is accustomed to short cuts to learning and demands that his information shall be presented in condensed form, will no longer brook the long-winded investigations, so often ending only in impotent conclusions, which delighted the leisurely Athenians Unlike modern writers, who discreetly conceal the process by which opinions have been reached, our author takes us, as it were, into his confidence, proclaiming openly that his own mind is not yet made up, and that he, like ourselves, is only groping after truth. Thus he not only records the tentative or contradictory propositions of those whose ideas he is drawing forth, but he lays bare his own hesitations and uncertainties, his own doubts and waverings. It is as if some poet should present for our perusal the first rough draft of his manuscript with all its erasures and corrections. "There are cases," says Grote, "in which two chemists have carried on joint researches, with many failures and disappointments, perhaps at last without success. If a record were preserved of their parley during the investigation, the grounds for testing and rejecting one conjecture and for selecting what should be tried after it, this would be in many points a parallel to the Platonic process."[1] And yet it should not fail to be recognized that "the soul of Plato's thought is present entire at every point in the body of his work, and it is not safe to touch an iota subscript of his text without being aware of this."[2] It behooves us, therefore, to use extreme caution in affirming of any apparent inconsistency that it is radical or irreconcilable.

[1] Grote's *Plato*, vol. i. p. 240.
[2] Paul Shorey, *Class. Rev.*, vol. iv. p. 480.

Although certain parts of Plato's dialogues may strike us to-day as obscure or obsolete, it is impossible to read them without being impressed by the modernness of their thought. We are constantly startled by passages which bear as directly upon questions of our own day as if they were written by one conversant with the latest phase of nineteenth-century life. The truth is that we are indebted to Plato for more than we know. Like the man who found in Shakspeare nothing but a collection of quotations, we are constantly recognizing in him thoughts long familiar to ourselves. "Out of Plato," says Emerson, "come all the thoughts that are still written and debated among men of thought. Great havoc makes he among our originalities. We have reached the mountain from which all these drift boulders were detached. The Bible of the learned for twenty-two centuries, every brisk young man who says in succession fine things to each reluctant generation is some reader of Plato translating into the vernacular, wittily, his good things."[1] Doubtless the masterly realism with which the personages of the Platonic drama are portrayed, the wonderful touches of that nature which makes all centuries akin, contribute in large measure to this sense of modernness which blends and yet contrasts curiously with these pictures of old Greek life, with its pleasant daily meetings in Agora and palaestra, its limitless time for social chat and philosophic discussion, its frequent allusions to contemporaneous persons and events.

Before we turn to the scenes which are to be enacted before us, let us make the acquaintance of the chief characters about to figure there. Two at least of these are already known to readers familiar with the *Apology* or the *Crito*. Although the parts assigned them here are insignificant, the actors are at once to be recognized, — Chaerephon by

[1] *Representative Men.*

the eager impetuosity of his greeting to Socrates on his return from camp,[1] Crito by the prudent fear lest his friend commit an undignified act by going to school with boys, and by the cautious wish to know beforehand exactly what he is to learn from the Sophist brothers, Euthydemus and Dionysodorus.[2] This singular pair of claimants to universal knowledge need not here be presented, as they will best be made known to us later through their own words. Ctesippus, the clever young fellow, "with all the impetuosity of his years,"[3] is admirably adapted to enter the lists against such antagonists as these. Stopping at no absurdity, he does his best to surpass their extravagances, and more than once succeeds in turning the laugh against them.

In striking contrast to the two brothers, follows, in the next dialogue, the grave and dignified teacher of the young Theaetetus, — Theodorus the geometrician. Disclaiming any knowledge outside of his own special study, he is yet sufficiently acquainted with the views of the Heracliteans to be stirred to wrath at the bare mention of the loose thinkers whom his exact soul abhors, and whom he characterizes as "admitting nothing fixed, whether in argument or in their own souls."[4] The cautious conservatism with which he avoids taking any active part in the discussion — a caution which the other two collocutors lose no opportunity to override — is as characteristic a trait of Theodorus as is, on the part of Socrates, the eager proffer of himself "to be killed and boiled," if need be, provided only he be turned out a good man.[5]

The character of Critias, in the *Charmides*, although it gives no premonition of his subsequent career, is not so much softened as to lose its value as a portrait. His self-esteem and love of approbation are amusingly played off by

---

[1] *Charmides*, 153 B–C.   [2] *Euthydemus*, 272 B–D.
[3] *Ibid.* 273 A.   [4] *Theaetetus*, 180 B.   [5] *Euthydemus*, 285 C.

his young ward Charmides, under the guise of deference and submissiveness.

The fact that the chief actors in the *Laches* are historical personages lends a peculiar interest to this dialogue. Prominent as generals no less than as citizens, Laches and Nicias differ as widely in regard to their common interest, the art of warfare, as in their traits of character. That Laches is both a good lover and a good hater is shown by his whole-souled admiration of Socrates and by his round abuse of the cautious and prudent Nicias, who in his turn does not scruple to express in unflattering terms his opinion of his adversary's ability. The spirit of recrimination betrayed in the remarks of both is set off by the calm and dispassionate manner in which Socrates conducts his investigations. The fiery and impatient Laches is, with somewhat questionable consistency, made the mouthpiece of one of Plato's most characteristic and beautiful descriptions, — that of the true musician whose life is attuned to a noble harmony of words and deeds, — a passage which has been called the keynote of Plato's theory of virtue.[1]

But it is of a younger generation that the most vivid as well as the most attractive portraits are drawn. In the *Laches*, it is true, the boys whose education is the objective point of the conversation play only a passive part; but in each of the other dialogues the figures upon whom our attention centres belong to the flower of the Athenian youth, and bear that stamp of breeding which seems to have been a birthright of noble parentage, and which goes far to justify the aristocratic predilections of Plato. Free from concern as to their own reputation, they have no thought of concealing the "wonder" which Socrates prizes as an "affection peculiar to the philosophic mind."[2] All alike display a charming

[1] *Laches*, 188 C–E.   [2] *Theaetetus*, 155 D.

simplicity and ingenuousness, which are the more remarkable by reason of the adulation lavished upon them by young and old. It speaks well for the healthiness and symmetry of Hellenic influences that a universal adoration, partaking almost of a religious character, has imparted to them no trace of vanity or self-consciousness, the taint of which must inevitably have diminished their zeal in the pursuit of truth.

There is Cleinias, the lad in whose future welfare, as scion of an illustrious family, his fellow citizens feel so deep an interest.[1] Led by the kindly guidance of Socrates, he is released from his painful bewilderment, and enabled to form by himself such sound conclusions that he no longer, it is declared, "needs either Euthydemus or any one else to teach him."[2] There is Lysis, with his shy impulsiveness, his artless candour, his absorbed interest in the discussion, and his insatiable eagerness to hear "more besides;"[3] and the maturer Menexenus, his bosom friend, a terrible fellow for pugnacity, as Socrates playfully pretends to know to his cost.[4] And pre-eminent among all is the gracious figure of Charmides, beautiful in mind as in body, an enchanting combination of modest dignity and arch sprightliness.

But as the *Theaetetus* is of these five dialogues the most serious and profound, so the chief personage there depicted is the best calculated to excite our admiration and interest. Although the physical beauty of the other youths has been denied him, he is yet one of the most attractive of the group. Much as we are led to expect from the enthusiastic description which precedes his appearance, his own revelation to us of his character and intellect does not disappoint us. The very embodiment of unobtrusive modesty, he is yet full of courage in the expression of his opinions, and ever ready

---

[1] *Euthydemus*, 275 A.   [2] *Ibid.* 290 E.
[3] *Lysis*, 211 B.   [4] *Ibid.* 211 C.

to throw himself into the breach and assume a part which he would fain have seen filled by another. "You are a beauty, Theaetetus," Socrates exclaims, "for he who speaks beautiful words is himself both beautiful and good."[1] There is a peculiar pathos in the contrast between the bright future predicted for Theaetetus and the touching picture of this noble youth mortally wounded and on his way home to die.

The allusion to the battle which decided the fate of Theaetetus,[2] probably that which took place late in the summer of 394 B. C., would fix this date as the one assumed for the dialogue, just as the reference to the fight at Potidaea[3] (432 B. C.) leaves no doubt as to the supposed date of the *Charmides*. A clew is given also as to the time of action of the *Laches* by the mention of the battle of Delium (424 B. C.) as a past occurrence,[4] while an allusion to Alcibiades the Older as dead[5] (404 B. C.) assigns certain limits of time to the *Euthydemus*. Every student of Plato, however, knows that, although historical allusions of this kind are of great value in fixing a time prior to which the dialogue in question could not have been composed, we must be very cautious about drawing any rash conclusions from the juxtaposition in which persons and events are placed, for our author allows no questions of consistency to hinder the free play of his imagination. Availing himself of the poet's privilege to subordinate historical accuracy to dramatic truth, he never hesitates, if it suits his purpose, to make his actors take part in events which occurred before they were born, or to allude to incidents which did not take place till long after their death.

It may also here be noted that, although in the dramatic portions of Plato's dialogues, every word of Socrates, if not actually taken from his lips, is at least such as he might have

---

[1] *Theaetetus*, 185 E. [2] *Ibid.* 142 B. [3] *Charmides*, 153 B.
[4] *Laches*, 181 B. [5] *Euthydemus*, 275 A.

uttered, we find, in passing to the philosophical discussions, that "the Socrates of these discourses is in great measure Plato himself, expounding — under his master's name and with much of his master's manner — doctrines of his own which he had developed under the inspiration of the teachings of Socrates, or which he believed Socrates would have approved if he could have lived to appreciate them. We have, in fact, here suddenly passed from the Socratic to the Platonic Socrates. Plato was in the habit of using his master in his dialogues as a mouthpiece for the expression of his own speculations; and he thus makes him utter many doctrines which the real Socrates would hardly have understood, and many which that rigid questioner would have subjected to a merciless cross-examination. . . . Still we must remember that it is through Plato that his master is best known; and it is the Platonic Socrates, quite as much as the real Socrates who has passed into history. Even Aristotle often quotes Plato's doctrines under the name of Socrates."[1]

In the *Theaetetus*, various schools of philosophy, both past and present, are successively passed in review; and their leaders, even when not referred to by name, were doubtless easily identified by an audience to many of whom they must have been personally known. For none except for Parmenides, the great chief of the Eleatic school, who taught that all existence is one and changeless, does Socrates, or Plato in his name, express any respect.[2] Protagoras is treated with the same good-natured and amused tolerance as elsewhere;[3] while in the *Euthydemus*, Isocrates, whom Plato chooses to regard as a type of the half-way philosopher, desiring to keep clear of risks and at the same time to reap every attainable advantage, is so severely dealt with that by his side even the

---

[1] Professor Goodwin's Introduction to *Socrates*.
[2] *Theaetetus*, 183 E.   [3] *Ibid.* 161 B–168 C.

Sophist Euthydemus for once appears to advantage.[1] The spirit of compromise never received a sterner rebuke than in this scathing denunciation.

In the Sophist brothers, already several times alluded to, Plato draws an amusing caricature of a type to whom he has been accused of doing scant justice. That the Sophists were simply the average teachers of the day, representing neither more nor less than the average standard of morality, is now too well established to need further demonstration. In professing to impart virtue and wisdom, they were really not professing to impart what Plato himself understood by these terms, for to them wisdom meant practical knowledge of affairs, while virtue meant mere efficiency in public and private life. Thus their pretentious promises, which enticed men away from nobler studies and pursuits, were not necessarily made with intent to deceive. But to an idealist like Plato it was a debasement of terms to class among those who had embraced the high calling of teacher, men to whom ethical doctrine was an accessory rather than a primary purpose, and who regarded as of subordinate interest that which, in ironical phase, he describes as "the one little thing beside ... a noble soul."[2] That the effort to "grow like unto God" in justice, wisdom, and holiness[3] should be abandoned for the accomplishment of some "slavish task,"[4] that truth should be disregarded,—truth, the "knowledge of which is wisdom and true virtue, while the ignorance of it is sheer stupidity and vice,"[5]—this in his eyes was the unpardonable offence of all. It is for this reason that he does not scruple here as elsewhere to expose to ridicule the overweening pretensions to knowledge and the utter incompetency of the men

---

[1] *Euthydemus*, 305 C–306 D.   [2] *Charmides*, 154 D.
[3] *Theaetetus*, 176 B.   [4] *Ibid.* 175 E.   [5] *Ibid.* 176 C.

whom he has chosen as the personification of false teaching. The famous irony of Socrates was never more characteristically or amusingly displayed than when, under pretence of admiring their skill and cleverness, he makes the brothers Euthydemus and Dionysodorus give an exhibition of their manner of "refuting every proposition whether it happen to be true or false,"[1] which exhibition is in itself the most complete argument against their own method.

If there is room for wonder that fallacies the grotesqueness of which is to us so palpable should have been tolerated, nay, even enthusiastically received, by any intelligent audience, it should yet be remembered that "the wisest of men are limited by the conditions of the age in which they live."[2] The various sophisms of which Plato here gives us the *reductio ad absurdum* may not unfairly be classed among other "erroneous tendencies of the reasoning process frequently incident to human thought and speech, — specimens of those ever renewed inadvertencies of ordinary thinking which it is the peculiar mission of philosophy, or reasoned truth, to rectify."[3] Nor must we forget that even "in modern times there is no fallacy so gross, no trick of language so transparent, no abstraction so barren and unmeaning, no form of thought so contradictory to experience, which has not been found to satisfy the minds of philosophical inquirers at a certain stage, or when regarded from a certain point of view only. The peculiarity of the fallacies of our own age is that we live within them, and are therefore generally unconscious of them."[4]

To bring to any formal conclusion the ever-renewed search

---

[1] *Euthydemus*, 272 B.
[2] Jowett's Introduction to Purves' *Selections from Plato*.
[3] Grote's *Plato*, vol. i. p. 550.
[4] Jowett's Introduction to *Euthydemus*.

for truth was assuredly far from the purpose of one who esteemed search a greater good than knowledge. But we shall find that in Plato's dialogues the discussion is rarely brought to a close without the introduction of some new thought which has perhaps a more practical value than the problem originally proposed. From the *Charmides* we have obtained, it is true, no definition of temperance, — a name which, like justice in the Republic, stands for the highest ideal of virtue, — but we have learned that for the attainment of that ideal no one particular quality can suffice. To be moderate, to be prudent, or even to possess that knowledge of self which, in Plato's estimation, is the foundation of all knowledge, is not sufficient for perfect temperance. Only by the possession of virtue in its integrity can be brought about the harmonious union between body and soul which makes life itself a harmony sweeter than that of "lute or any instrument for pastime."[1] And so in the *Lysis*, where, descending to a less lofty plane, we deal with human relationships, the very failure of the attempt to define so familiar a thing as friendship teaches the salutary lesson that to accept or take for granted is not the same as to know, and that what we suppose ourselves to know best we are often most ignorant of. Again in the *Laches*, although we fail to gain any adequate conception of courage, we learn to estimate the uselessness of any special knowledge compared with that larger wisdom which is reached only through contemplating the great problems of life, — a self-education which ends not with the passing away of childhood, but must needs be pursued so long as life itself shall last.[2]

By exemplifying a vain show of knowledge, the *Euthydemus* paves the way for the genuine search which is undertaken in the last of the dialogues before us. The *Theaetetus*

[1] *Laches*, 188 D.   [2] *Ibid.* 188 B.

bears, it has been said, the same relation to Plato's theory of knowledge as the *Gorgias* to his theory of morals. One of the most highly finished and perfect in form of the Platonic dialogues, it ranks also as "the most exact in philosophic expression," and is pregnant with the deepest thought. What is perhaps its most important contribution to philosophy — the discovery that the soul of man is a central principle by which alone perception is transformed into thought — excited among its first hearers an enthusiasm which may appear unwarranted by a proposition so familiar to ourselves. So true it is that "the highest effort of philosophy in one generation may become the common sense of the next,"[1] and that what to-day stands in the light of a mere truism was little short of a revelation in the eyes of those to whom it threw open a whole world of new ideas.

But Plato does not long confine his subject to a purely intellectual plane. Since to his mind right conduct is inseparable from right knowledge, the moral aspect cannot be far from view, and we soon find ourselves contemplating the ever recurring struggle between the two living types, — the phantom of perception, falsely called Real; and the Ideal, the only true reality. The "digression"[2] wherein the "two ways of living" are contrasted and the choice of the higher is justified is filled with a solemn beauty which recalls a similar passage in the *Republic*, where the few "noble natures" and "great souls" whose "thoughts are fixed upon realities"[3] are likened to "one who, overtaken by a mighty tempest and storm of dust swept onward by the wind, shelters himself behind a wall, rejoicing if he may pass through his earthly life free from evil deeds and unrighteousness, and on

---

[1] Jowett's Introduction to Purves' *Selections from Plato*.
[2] *Theaetetus*, 172 C–177 C.
[3] *Republic*, 500 B.

his release, depart hence filled with fair hopes and good will to all." [1]

It is interesting to observe that the motives adduced for right action imply a spiritual conception of the future life. The incentive to "become just, holy, and wise withal" is that, since the man "who has made himself the most just" is most like him who himself is "perfectly just," we shall thus "grow like unto God," and so find the "way of escape hence to yonder place." The "reward of unrighteousness" to be dreaded is that we shall "grow in the likeness of that which we resemble," and may not therefore hope, "when dead, to be received into that place which is free from evil." [2] It is surely not fanciful to trace throughout this beautiful passage of the *Theaetetus* a foreshadowing of the triumphant vindication soon to be shown forth in the trial and death of Socrates, a fit ending to a life wherein "words are attuned to deeds," [3] — such a life as is "lived by gods and by men blessed of Heaven." [4]

[1] *Republic*, 496 D-E.
[2] *Theaetetus*, 176 A-177 A.
[3] *Laches*, 188 D.
[4] *Theaetetus*, 176 A.

CONTENTS.

	PAGE
CHARMIDES	3
LYSIS	23
LACHES	41
EUTHYDEMUS	63
THEAETETUS	99
NOTES	149

CHARMIDES.

CHARMIDES.

CHARACTERS.

SOCRATES.
CHAEREPHON, *a friend of* SOCRATES.
CHARMIDES, *a young Athenian.*
CRITIAS, *guardian of* CHARMIDES.

The scene is laid in the Palaestra of TAUREAS.

TALKS WITH ATHENIAN YOUTHS.

CHARMIDES.

I RETURNED last evening from the camp at Potidaea,[1] and was well pleased after so long an absence to visit my familiar haunts again. I looked in of course at the palaestra of Taureas, which is right opposite the temple of Basile;[2] and there I found a very large company, some unknown to me, but for the most part old friends. The sight of me took them by surprise, and while I was still at a distance they began, each from where he sat, to bid me welcome. Chaerephon,[3] however, like the crazy-brained fellow that he is, springing out from among them, ran to me and, seizing me by the hand, exclaimed: "Oh, Socrates, can it be that you are safely out of the battle?"

Shortly before we came away a battle had taken place at Potidaea, the news of which had only now arrived.

"Just as you see me," I replied.

"Nay," said he, "but the report here is that the battle was a very severe one, and that many of our best-known citizens perished there."

"And the report," I said, "is not far from true."

"And were you in the battle?" he asked.

"I was."

"Then," said he, "come here, and sit down and tell us all about it, for we have heard no accurate account as yet."

As he spoke, he led me to a seat beside Critias, the son of Callaeschrus.[4] So I sat down, and, after greeting Critias and the others, gave them all the news of the camp that they wanted, for each one had a different question to ask.

When we had had enough of this, I in my turn asked them for news of the city,—how it fared now with matters of philosophy, and whether any of our youths had become noted for their intellect or their beauty, or for both. Just then Critias, looking toward the door, saw a number of young fellows coming in, laughing and making jokes together, while a crowd of others brought up the rear.

"As to beauties, Socrates," he said, "you will soon, I imagine, see for yourself; for these who are now coming in are the followers and lovers of the youth who passes for the most beautiful of the present day, and he himself I presume is on his way here and already close at hand."

"Who is he?" I asked, "and who is his father?"

"You probably know him yourself," he replied, "only he was not grown up when you went away, — my cousin Charmides, the son of my uncle Glaucon."[5]

"By Zeus!" I exclaimed, "of course I know him. Even then, as a child, he was not one to be passed unnoticed, but now I suppose he must be a well-grown lad."

"You shall see directly how large he is, and what he has grown to be."

The words were yet on his lips when Charmides entered. Now, my friend, you cannot judge by me, for in regard to beauty I am simply like a chalk-mark upon a white wall; almost any one in the bloom of youth appears to me beautiful. But still, this lad did strike me as a marvel, both as to beauty and stature; and it seemed to me that the rest of the company were one and all in love with him, from the flutter and commotion that greeted his entrance; while a crowd of other admirers followed in his train. Now this was less surprising with men of our own age, but I noticed that among the boys also there was not one — not even the very smallest — who looked in any other direction; all gazed upon him as if upon some sacred statue.[6] Then Chaerephon calling me by name, —

"Well, Socrates," said he, "what do you think of the youth? Is he not fair of face?"

"Marvellously fair," I answered.

"And yet," said he, "if he would but take off his garments you would think his face ill-favoured, so faultlessly beautiful is his form."

And all the others confirmed the words of Chaerephon.

"By Heracles!" I cried, "you make the fellow out irresistible, if he has only one little thing besides."

"What?" asked Critias.

"If he has a noble soul," I answered; "and this, in truth, Critias, he ought to have, since he is of your family."

"In this respect also," said Critias, "he is perfection itself."[7]

"What say you, then?" I asked; "shall we not take the vesture from off his soul and consider that, before his outward form? Doubtless at his age he is fond of conversation."

"Exceedingly so," Critias answered, "especially as he has a turn for philosophy, and in the opinion of some, himself included, is a good deal of a poet besides."

"This gift, dear Critias," said I, "is one which dates far back in your family, from your kinship with Solon.[8] But why will you not call the lad here and show him to me? There could be no harm — could there — in his conversing with us were he even younger than he is, when you, his guardian and cousin as well, are by?"

"You are quite right," he said, "and we will send for him."

With that, turning to the attendant, "Boy," he said, "go fetch Charmides; but first say that I wish to present him to a physician, for the cure of that ailment about which he was complaining to me the other day. He said," continued Critias, addressing me, "that of late his head had been feeling heavy when he got up in the morning. Now why should you not pretend that you know some sort of cure for his headache?"

"Why not indeed?" said I; "only let him come."

"Oh, he will come," said he.

And so it happened; for he did come, and was the cause of much merriment. We who were seated there began, in hot haste, every man to push his neighbour, in order that Charmides might sit by his side, until at last he who was seated at the one end was forced to get up, while he on the other fell over sideways. Charmides, meanwhile, came and sat down between Critias and myself.

Now by this time, my friend, I had already begun to be troubled, and the confidence I had felt, of being able to talk to him with perfect ease, was at an end. . . . However, when he asked if I knew the cure for the headache, I with much difficulty just managed to answer that I did.

"Well," he asked, "what is it?"

Whereupon I told him that it was a kind of leaf; and that, besides the remedy, there was a certain charm which, if pronounced at the same moment that the remedy was applied, effected a perfect cure; but that without the charm the leaf itself was of no avail." [9]

"I will write down the charm from your dictation," he said.

"Whether you can persuade me to let you or not?" I asked.

At this he laughed. "If I can persuade you, Socrates," he said.

"Very good," said I; "and are you quite sure of my name?"

"Yes, unless I am all in the wrong," he answered, "for you are not a little talked about by boys of our age; and then too I remember when I was a child seeing you with my cousin Critias."

"That is well," I said. "I shall speak to you with all the more freedom about the nature of the charm, for until now I have been at a loss how to show you the extent of its power. Such, Charmides, is its nature that it is not the head alone which it is capable of curing. Doubtless ere now you have heard our competent physicians say, when a man comes to them suffering from his eyes, that it is impossible to attempt the cure of the eyes alone, inasmuch as the head must be treated at the same time, if the eyes are ever to be cured; and so again with the head, to suppose that it may be treated by itself apart from the whole body would be sheer nonsense. Following out this principle, they apply the regimen to every part of the body, and make it their aim to treat and cure the whole, together with the part. Have you not noticed that this is what they say, and that it is really so?"

"Certainly I have," he said.

"And do you not think them right, and agree with them?"

"By all means," he said.

Being now sure of his approval I again took heart, and by degrees my confidence was restored and I felt renewed life within me. And I said,—

"Well, Charmides, of a like nature is this charm. I learned it yonder on the campaign from one of the physicians of the Thracian king Zamolxis, who also are said to confer immortality.[10] This Thracian told me that the Greek physicians are quite right in speaking as I have said. 'But Zamolxis,' he added, 'our King, who is moreover a God, says that just as the cure of the eyes should not be attempted without that of the head also, nor that of the head without the body, even so there is no cure for the body apart from the soul; and the reason why so many diseases elude the physicians of Greece is that they know nothing of the whole, which ought to be their chief care, since if this be not sound, it is impossible for any part to be well. For all things,' he declared, 'both bad and good, not only in the body but in every part of the man, have their starting-point in the soul, whence they overflow, in the same way as from the head into the eyes. First then and above all the soul must be treated, if the head and the rest of the body are ever to be made whole; and the cure of the soul,' he said, my boy, 'is brought about by means of certain charms, which charms are good words. By these words temperance is begotten in the soul; and, this once begotten and abiding there, it is easy enough to supply health to the head and the rest of the body.' And as he taught me the cure and the charms, 'Let no one,' he urged, 'persuade you to treat him for headache with this medicine, until he has first yielded up to you his soul to be treated by the charm. For just here,' he declared, 'the mistake is made in regard to men. They attempt to treat the body independently of the soul.' And most strenuously did he command me to let no man, were he ever so rich or well-born or fair, prevail upon me to do otherwise than this; whereupon I took my oath to him, and I must needs perform it, and so I will. And if you, following the stranger's injunctions, will first of all consent to yield up your soul to be charmed through the Thracian's charm, I will afterward apply the cure to the head. Otherwise, I know not what I could do for you, dear Charmides."

On hearing this, Critias exclaimed: "A godsend indeed, Socrates, would this headache prove to the boy, if for the sake of his head he should be compelled to improve his intellect. I can assure you, however, that Charmides has been held to surpass his fellows, not in outward form alone, but in this very quality for which you say you have a charm,—temperance you call it, do you not?"[11]

"Precisely that."

"Know then," he went on, "that he is accounted far the most temperate among our youths, and, considering his age, in all other respects inferior to none."

"And by good rights, Charmides," said I, "do you surpass others in all these respects, for I suppose there is no one here present who could readily point out two Athenian houses, the union of which was likely to bring forth a fairer and better descendant than those from which you are sprung. Your father's family, that of Critias, son of Dropidas, has been handed down to us in the eulogies of Anacreon and Solon and many other poets, as pre-eminent in beauty and virtue and whatever else is deemed a blessing. And it is the same on your mother's side, for of your uncle Pyrilampes it is said that often as he was sent on embassies to the great King, or anywhere else on the continent, no one in any place was ever held his superior, whether in beauty or in stature. Indeed, that whole house is no whit inferior to the other. Such being your ancestry, it is to be expected that you should be first in all things. And so far, dear son of Glaucon, as the eye judges of your outward form, you are, methinks, in no respect inferior to any of your predecessors. So that if, as our friend here assures us, you are well endowed with temperance and other virtues besides, then indeed, dear Charmides, your mother bore you to be blessed. The case, therefore, stands thus: If, as Critias here says, you have already acquired temperance, and are sufficiently temperate, you need no further charm, whether that of Zamolxis or of Abaris the Hyperborean,[12] but may be given at once the cure for headache. If, however, you still seem to come short of this, the charm must be used before the cure is applied. Tell me yourself, then, whether you agree with our friends, and think that you have a sufficient share of temperance already, or are you still lacking in this?"

Hereupon Charmides blushed and looked even lovelier than before, for this modesty of his well became his years. His answer, nevertheless, was not without dignity, for what he said was that, under the circumstances, it was not easy either to agree to the assertion or to deny it.

"For if I deny that I am temperate," said he, "not only is that an absurd thing for any one to say about himself, but I shall be making Critias out a liar, as well as many others who, according to him, hold me as temperate; if, on the other hand, I declare that I am temperate, I shall be praising myself, which is of course offensive; so that I really have no answer to give you."

"What you say, Charmides," I remarked, "seems to me reasonable; and I think we had best consider together whether you do possess the quality in question or not, in order that neither you may be forced into saying what you do not like, nor I into taking up the practice of medicine inconsiderately. If, therefore, it is agreeable to you, I should like to look into the matter with you; if not, we will let it go."

"I should like it of all things," he said; "so pray begin just where you think best."

[158 E.-162 A. In compliance with the request of Socrates, Charmides, after much hesitation, proposes two successive definitions of temperance. The first — calmness or repose — is rejected on the ground that most actions are better performed quickly than slowly. The second — modesty — reached after 'a right manly effort of mind,' is pronounced deficient, on the strength of a quotation from Homer to the effect that "modesty is no good thing for a needy man."[13] Charmides then bethinks him of another definition, — attending to one's own affairs. Upon this, Socrates exclaims, —

161 C. "Oh, you rogue, you got this from Critias here or from some other of the wise men."

"From some other most likely," Critias protests, "for it was certainly not from me."

"But what difference does it make," asks Charmides, "where I got it?"

"None at all," Socrates admits, "for of course we are not here to examine who said it, but whether or not it is true."

"You are right there," is the rejoinder.

"Of course I am; still I shall be surprised if we ever do find out the meaning, for it looks as if it were a sort of riddle."

After demonstrating, incidentally, that no one in a civilized community can be absolutely independent of other men, Socrates resumes as follows:]

162 A. "Well, as I said just now, he who defined temperance as attending to one's own business was speaking in riddles, for he was not, I presume, quite a fool; or perhaps it was some fool that told you, Charmides?"

"On the contrary," said he, "I supposed him to be particularly wise."

"Then most assuredly he was proposing it as a riddle, meaning how hard it is to know what attending to one's own business is."

"Very likely," said he.

"Well, what is it to attend to one's own business? Can you tell me?"

"Not I, by Zeus; and I really should not wonder if he who said this may not know himself what he meant." And as he spoke he glanced meaningly at Critias and smiled.

Now, it had been evident for some time past that Critias was getting uneasy, and anxious about sustaining his reputation before Charmides and the others, and that he had barely restrained himself up to this moment; but now he could do so no longer. And this makes me all the more certain that my suspicion was true, and that it was from Critias that Charmides had heard the answer concerning temperance. Charmides, however, who did not wish to undertake the defence of the definition himself, but to have Critias do it, kept urging him on and pointing out how he had been worsted in the argument. This was too much for Critias, and he got angry with Charmides, — just, I thought, as a poet might get angry with some actor who has recited his verses badly. Thus, looking him straight in the face, he said, —

"So you think, Charmides, do you, that just because you do not know what the man means who said that temperance is attending to one's own business, he himself, forsooth, does not know?"

"But, my excellent Critias," said I, "it is no wonder that Charmides, at his age, should know nothing about what you, with your superior age and experience, doubtless do understand. If you therefore agree that temperance is what he now calls it, and are ready to accept the definition, I would much rather examine with you whether or not it is true."

"I agree to it entirely," he said, "and I do accept the definition."

[162 E.–175 D. In imitation of the verbal hair-splitting of Prodicus,[14] Critias, to suit his own purpose, draws distinctions between *making*, *doing*, and *acting*, and quotes Hesiod's saying, "Work is no disgrace," in support of what he now proclaims to be his true meaning; namely, that temperance consists in the performance of good works, which, whether for one's self or for others, are a man's own or proper business; intemperance, in the performance of works which, being useless or ignoble, are of alien character.

But what, it is objected, if one be unconscious of his own temperance? As the physician cannot always know whether by healing a patient he is or is not conferring a benefit upon him, so a man, although acting with temperance or wisdom, may himself remain uncertain or even ignorant of it.

164 C. Critias now declares that he will own himself mistaken, rather than admit that a man who does not know himself can possess temperance; for that this is a quality inseparably linked with knowledge of self is shown by the coupling together in the Delphic temple of the two injunctions: Be temperate; Know thyself. He therefore proposes to substitute for the previous definition

that of self-knowledge. Here Socrates pauses to inquire into the purpose of temperance. As a science, it must be the science of something. What, then, is this thing? The answer is that, unlike other sciences, all of which are applied to an object outside of themselves, temperance, while including within itself all the other sciences, is pre-eminently the science of itself, its own reproduction being its legitimate end.

The demand for a more definite answer is met by a complaint from Critias that Socrates is trying to refute him.

166 C. "And if I do refute you," Socrates replies, "have I any motive save that which leads me to scrutinize my own words also,—the fear of unconsciously imagining myself to know when I do not know? And as to the search I am now making, it is chiefly indeed for myself, but for my other friends as well. For is it not a gain in which all men share, to have everything put in its true light?"

169 Further investigation arouses doubt as to the reality or use of such a science as the one just described, and a longing for the help of "some great man"[15] to solve it. 'And here,' Socrates remarks, 'Critias, hearing my words and beholding my perplexity, for all the world like those who, seeing their neighbour yawn, are themselves similarly affected, seemed himself also to have fallen a prey to perplexity. But, accustomed as he was to be treated with universal

deference, he was ashamed and unwilling before all the others to confess himself incapable of maintaining the point which I had challenged. So, to cover his perplexity, he muttered something quite unintelligible.'

Self-knowledge is finally abandoned as a definition of temperance, on the ground that it is an impossibility and that even if it were possible it would be useless.[16] One last attempt is made, by defining it as the knowledge of good and evil, but this also proves itself inadequate, and Socrates ends by confessing that he and his friends have been defeated in their attempt to define that quality which the " namer of things "[17] has called temperance or wisdom.]

175 D. "Now on my own account I am not so much troubled; but on yours, Charmides, I am truly distressed if with such an outward form and, yet more, with such temperance of soul, you are to derive no benefit from this temperance of yours, nor any help from its presence in your life. And still more am I distressed about the charm which I learned from the Thracian, if indeed that which I took such pains to acquire is in reality a thing of no worth. I do not, however, believe that this is actually the case, but rather that I myself am poor at searching; for tem-
176 perance is surely a great blessing, and if you really have it, happy are you. Consider, therefore, whether you do possess it and have no

need of the charm. For, if you do, I would advise you rather to account me a foolish babbler, incapable of finding out anything at all with the help of reason, if you will only believe that the more you grow in temperance the happier you will be."

Then Charmides said: "By Zeus, Socrates, I do not know whether I possess it or not. How, indeed, should I know a thing, the nature of which even you are incapable of ascertaining? At least this is what you say, though I do not much believe you. But as for myself, Socrates, I do think that I am in great need of the charm; and there is no reason, so far as I am concerned, why I should not let myself be charmed by you every day, until you say that it is enough."

"That is well, Charmides," said Critias; "only do this and I shall deem it a proof of your temperance, that you give yourself up to be charmed by Socrates, and never desert him in great matters or in small."

"Rest assured," he answered, "that I shall follow him and never be a deserter. Indeed, I should be doing a dreadful thing to disobey you who are my guardian, and not do as you command."

"Well, I do command it," Critias said.

"Then I shall do it," he said, "beginning from this very day."

"Come now," said I, "what are you two plotting about?"

"Nothing," said Charmides; "our plots are already laid."

"So you are going to use force, are you," I asked, "and not let me even present my case?"

"Yes, you must expect force," he replied, "since Critias here commands; therefore you had best be considering what you will do about it."

"But there is no longer any use in considering," said I; "for if you have made up your mind to accomplish anything, no matter what, and that by force to boot, no human being is capable of opposing you."

"Then do not you oppose me either," he said.

"Indeed I shall not," I answered.

LYSIS.

LYSIS.

CHARACTERS.

SOCRATES.
LYSIS,
MENEXENUS, } *young Athenians.*
HIPPOTHALES, *an admirer of* LYSIS.
CTESIPPUS *of Pacania.*

The scene is laid in a newly built Palaestra, just outside the walls of Athens.

LYSIS.

I was walking straight across from the Academy to the Lyceum, by the outside road close under the wall,[1] when, on reaching the little gate by the fountain of Panops, I met Hippothales the son of Hieronymus, and Ctesippus the Paeanian, and several other youths gathered together in a group.[2] As he saw me approaching, Hippothales called out,—

"Ho, Socrates, where are you from, and whither bound?"

"I have come from the Academy and am going straight across to the Lyceum," I answered.

"Come straight here instead," he cried. "Why not turn aside to us? It is worth your while, I can tell you."

"Where, pray?" I asked; "and whom do you mean by 'us'?"

"Here," he said, pointing to an enclosed space with an open door, right opposite the wall. "Here is where we spend our time; and not we only, but many others, and handsome fellows too."

"But what is this place, and how do you spend your time in it?"

"It is a newly built palaestra," he replied; "and our time is spent for the most part in conversation, of which we would gladly give you a share."

"Very kind of you," said I; "and who is the teacher there?"

"Your friend and admirer, Miccus," he answered.

"By Zeus!" I exclaimed, "he is no ordinary man,—in fact, an accomplished Sophist."

"Will you come with us then," he asked, "and see for yourself who are there?"

[204 B.–206 D. Still another motive for visiting the palaestra is shortly presented. A certain fair and well-born youth, Lysis by name, is greatly beloved by Hippothales, who, as shown by a humorous account from Ctesippus, has so overwhelmed the object of his admiration with praise and adulation, that he has made himself odious to the modest youth. Conscious of his own want of success, Hippothales appeals to Socrates to know by what word or course of action he may best ingratiate himself.]

"That is not easy to tell," I replied. "If, however, you cared to have him converse with me, I might perhaps be able to give you an example of what I think you ought to say to him, instead of the verses and songs in which your friends here tell me you address him."

"No difficulty about that," he said. "If you

and Ctesippus here will go inside and sit down for a talk together, he will, I think, join you of his own accord; for he is especially fond, Socrates, of listening. And besides, as they are celebrating the Hermaea,[3] the young men and boys are allowed to mingle together, so he is sure to join you. But if he does not, he is well acquainted with Ctesippus, through Menexenus, who is a cousin of Ctesippus and, as it happens, the most intimate friend of Lysis. Therefore if he does not come to you of his own accord, Ctesippus shall summon him."

"Yes," I said, "that is the best way."

Herewith, taking hold of Ctesippus, I went into the palaestra, the others bringing up the rear.

On entering we found that the sacred rites were nearly over, and that the boys, all in their festive array, had offered the sacrifices and were having a game at knuckle-bones. The greater part of them were in the court outside; but in a corner of the disrobing-room [4] a few were playing at odd and even, with a quantity of bones which they took out of little wicker baskets. A group of lookers-on surrounded them. Among these was Lysis, who, with a chaplet upon his head, shone out pre-eminent among the boys and youths, and seemed worthy of note, not for beauty alone, but for graces of character as well. As for us, we withdrew to the opposite side, and sitting down (for it was quiet there), entered into conversation. Now Lysis kept turning round to look at us, evidently longing to draw near. For a while, however, he was at a loss what to do, as he hesitated to come forward alone. But by-and-by, Menexenus, in the midst of his game, came in from the court, and seeing Ctesippus and myself, came over and sat down by us. As soon as Lysis saw this, he followed him and sat down too by the side of Menexenus. Thereupon all the others came in also, and Hippothales among them, when he saw what a crowd was gathered there. But, so fearful was he of annoying Lysis, that he placed himself where he thought he should be concealed by the others and escape observation. Standing in this position, he listened.

Then, looking at Menexenus: "Which of you two, son of Demophon," I asked, "is the elder?"

"There is a dispute between us as to that," he answered.

"And you might dispute also, I suppose," said I, "which is the nobler?"

"Certainly we might."

"And which the handsomer?"

At this they both began to laugh.

"As to which is the richer," I said, "I shall not inquire; for you are friends, are you not?"

"That we are," they replied.

"And friends, they say, have all things in common; so that in this respect at least there will be no difference between you,—that is, if you speak the truth about your friendship."

They assented.

I was on the point of asking which was the juster and which the wiser of the two; but before I had time, some one came in for Menexenus, saying that the director of the gymnasium was calling for him, as it was, I believe, his turn to offer some sacrifice. So he went off, and I fell to questioning Lysis.

"I suppose, Lysis," said I, "that your father and mother love you very dearly?"

"Indeed they do," he said.

"And they would like to have you as happy as possible?"

"Of course they would!"

"Well, do you think any one happy, who is a slave and is never allowed to do what he wishes?"

"Not I, by Zeus," he replied.

"And since your father and mother love you and want you to become happy, it is evident, is it not, that they strive in every way to make you happy?"

"Of course they do!" he said.

"And so they allow you to do just as you please, and never scold you or prevent you from doing whatever you may wish?"

"In faith, Socrates, but they do; they prevent me very often."

"What do you mean?" I cried. "They wish

208 your happiness, and yet prevent your doing what you wish? Tell me, pray; if, during a race, you wanted to mount one of your father's chariots and take the reins, would they not allow you,— would they hinder you from doing it?"

"By Zeus," exclaimed he, "they would never allow me!"

"Whom then would they allow?"

"My father has a charioteer, to whom he pays a wage."

"What! they allow a hireling rather than you to do whatever he likes with the horses, and they give him money over and above?"

"Why not, pray?" he asked.

"But they do, I suppose, trust you to manage the pair of mules; and if you wished to take the whip and beat them, they would allow that?"

"Allow me, indeed!" he said.

"What!" I asked, "is no one allowed to beat them?"

"Oh yes, of course," said he; "the mule-driver."

"Is he a slave or a free man?"

"A slave."

"They think more then, it seems, of a slave than of you, their son! They entrust their possessions to him rather than to you, and allow him to do what he likes, while you they prevent! Well, tell me yet further. Do they give you the control of yourself, or do they not trust you even thus far?"

"Trust me indeed!"

"What! does some one else control you?"

"Yes, my tutor here."

"Not a slave, surely?"

"Why not?" he said. "He belongs to us."

"Well, it is a hard thing," I said, "that you, who are free-born, should be controlled by a slave. And in what way does this tutor of yours control you?"

"He takes me to my teacher's, of course."

"But surely, they, your teachers, do not also control you?"

"Assuredly they do."

"Well, your father seems nothing loath to set plenty of rulers and masters over you! Of course, however, when you come home to your mother, she, thinking only of your happiness, allows you to do whatever you like with the wool or the web, when she is weaving? Nor does she, I imagine, hinder you from disturbing the shuttle or the comb, or any of the other weaving implements?"

"By Zeus!" he answered, laughing; "not only does she prevent me, but if I were so much as to touch them, I should get a beating."

"By Heracles!" I cried; "surely you have never done an injury to your father or mother?"

"Not I, by Zeus!" he answered.

"Then for what reason, pray, do they prevent you so harshly from being happy and doing what you like, and keep you the whole day long enslaved to others, — in a word, doing hardly anything that you wish; insomuch that you apparently get no good from all your possessions, which every one else has more control over than yourself, — nor even from your own body, fair as it is, since this too is taken in charge and governed by another; while you, Lysis, have control of nothing, nor do anything that you desire?"

"Because I am not old enough yet, Socrates," he said.

"That would not prevent, son of Democrates," said I; "for there are cases, I imagine, where your father and mother do trust you, without waiting till you are old enough. When for instance they want some one to read or write for them, it is you, I presume, that they call upon to do this, rather than any other member of the household; is it not?"

"To be sure," he answered.

"And you are free, are you not, to choose which letters shall be written first, and which second in order, and the same in reading? And when you take your lyre, neither your father nor your mother, I presume, hinders you from loosening or tightening such of the strings as you choose, or from playing with your fingers, or striking with the plectrum,[5] — or do they hinder you in this?"

"Certainly not."

"And what, Lysis, can be their reason for not

hindering you here, when they do so in the matters of which we first spoke?"

"I suppose," said he, "it is because in the one case I understand, and in the other I do not."

"Oh, that is it, my dear fellow!" said I. "Your father then is not waiting for you to be of the right age to be trusted with all these things; but the first day he thinks your judgment better than his own, he will entrust to you not only the care of his property but of himself.

. . . .

210 A. "The case then, dear Lysis, stands thus. In matters which we understand all will trust us, — Greeks and barbarians, men and women alike, — and here we shall do as we please, and none will purposely hinder us, but we shall be free ourselves, and have control of others also; and these things will belong to us, for we shall get the good of them. But in matters which we do not understand no one will trust us to do as we like, but all will hinder us, so far as they can, — not strangers only, but father and mother, and one yet nearer than these if there be any such; and we shall be subject to others; and these things will not belong to us, for we shall get no good from them. Do you agree that this is so?"

"I do."

"And shall we be friends to any one, or will any one love us in respect to the matters wherein we are useless?"

"Certainly not."

"Then neither does your father love you, nor in fact does any one love any one else in so far as you or he is useless."

"It seems not."

"If you therefore, my boy, are wise, all men will be your friends and all as your kindred, for you will be useful and good. If not, there is no one, not even father or mother or kinsman, who will be your friend. Now then, Lysis, is it possible to pride one's self upon a knowledge of subjects of which one has no knowledge?"

"How could it be possible?" he answered.

"And if you still require a teacher, you have as yet no knowledge?"

"Very true."

"And if you have no knowledge you cannot pride yourself upon knowing?"

"By Zeus, Socrates," he cried, "I do not think I can."

On hearing this I glanced at Hippothales and came very near making a mistake, for I was on the point of saying, — "This, Hippothales, is the way to talk to your favourite, humbling him and setting him down, instead of flattering and spoiling him as you do." But when I perceived how confused and distressed he was by what had been said, I remembered that he had wished his presence kept a secret from Lysis; so I checked myself and refrained from speech.

Meanwhile Menexenus came back, and sat down again beside Lysis, in the place he had previously left. Then Lysis, in a most winning and affectionate way, whispered softly in my ear, so that Menexenus might not hear, —

"Do, Socrates, tell Menexenus also what you have been telling me."

"Tell him yourself, Lysis," I said, "for you have been paying close attention."

"Indeed I have," he said.

"Try your best then," said I, "to recall it, that you may give him an exact account of it all; and if there is anything you forget, you may ask me about it the next time we meet."

"Yes, Socrates," he said, "I certainly will, you may depend upon it. But do tell him something besides, so that I may listen also until it is time to go home."

"Well," I said, "I suppose I must, since you bid me. But mind that you come to my rescue if Menexenus attempts to overthrow me. Or perhaps you do not know that he is pugnacious?"

"That he is, by Zeus!" said he; "excessively so. And that is just why I want you to argue with him."

"That I may make myself ridiculous?" I asked.

"Oh no, indeed," he answered, "but that you may give him a lesson."

"How could I?" I cried. "No easy matter that, for he is a terrible fellow, — a pupil of Ctesippus, who by the way is here himself. Do you not see him?"

"Pay no attention to any one else, Socrates," he said, "but come and argue with him."

"It shall be done," I said.

As we talked thus together, Ctesippus called out, —

"Why are you two feasting there all by yourselves, and giving us no share in the talk?"

"Why, of course," said I, "you must have a share. This boy here does not quite understand something I have been telling him, but says he thinks Menexenus knows about it, and bids me ask him."

"Well," said he, "why don't you ask?"

"I am going to ask," I said; "and do you, Menexenus, answer what I am about to ask you. You must know that from childhood there is one thing that I have coveted, just as all men do covet, some one thing, some another, — one man for instance horses, another dogs; one wealth, another honour. Now, things of that kind I am indifferent about; but I have a passion for gaining friends, and would much rather get a good friend than the best cock or quail in the world. Yes, by Zeus, rather than a horse or a dog either! By the Dog,[6] I verily believe that I would choose a friend, before all the gold of Darius even, so great a lover of friends am I. When therefore I behold you two, Lysis and yourself, I am struck with amazement, and think what good fortune it is for you, young as you are, to have been able with such speed and ease to acquire this treasure, and to gain, each for himself, quickly yet surely, such a friend as you find in Lysis, and he in you. For my own part, so far am I from such a possession that I do not even know how one man becomes the friend of another; and it is precisely in regard to this that I want to question you, as one having experience."

[212 A.–221 E. The inquiry which ensues leads to the following question from Socrates:
213 C. "Whom then," he asks, "may we call friends one to the other?"

"By Zeus, Socrates," is the answer, "I for my part cannot very well make out."

"May it not be then, Menexenus," Socrates asks, "that we have not made our search at all in the right way?"

"I do not believe you have, Socrates," Lysis exclaims, blushing as he speaks; 'for so absorbed was he in the conversation — as he had evidently been from the first — that the words seemed to have escaped him involuntarily. Wishing to let Menexenus rest, and pleased with the earnestness shown by Lysis,' Socrates finishes with him the inquiry as to the true basis of friendship, the result of which is as follows:]

"If then," said I, "you are friends one to the other, there must be some sort of congeniality in your natures."

"Most assuredly," they both exclaimed.

"And if any one longs for another or loves him, you may be sure, my boys, that he could 222 never have felt this longing, or love, or friendship, if there had not been some congeniality in the soul, or in some quality of it, — either its moral character or habits or general type."

"Of course," said Menexenus.

But Lysis was silent.

"Very good," said I; "and it has been proved that we must necessarily love what is of a nature congenial to our own."

"So it seems," he said.

"Therefore he who unfeignedly loves, not he who merely pretends to love, must of necessity be loved by his beloved."

To this Lysis and Menexenus gave but faint assent, while Hippothales turned all colours for joy.

[222 B.–E. Further investigation, however, brings about the discovery that things of like nature cannot be mutually useful, and, after one more fruitless attempt at a satisfactory definition, Socrates thus recapitulates the steps already taken:]

"If then neither they who love nor they who are loved, neither the like nor the unlike, neither those who are good nor those who are of kin, nor any of the others we have passed in review, — I cannot remember them for their number, — if none of these, I say, are examples of friendship, why then I know not what more I can say."

223   With these words I had thought to stir up some one of the elders. But just then, like some kind of evil spirit, in came the tutors of Menexenus and Lysis,[7] with the brothers of the boys, and, calling out, ordered them to go straight home; for by this time it was late. At first we and the bystanders were for driving them off. As they, however, paid us no heed, but went on storming and shouting, with their outlandish accent, as loudly as ever, we came to the conclusion that they had been drinking a trifle at the Hermaea, and would be hard to deal with; so that, fairly worsted by them, we broke up the assembly. But as they were going off, I said, —

"In truth, Lysis and Menexenus, we have been cutting a ridiculous figure, — I, old man that I am, and you along with me. For these people will go off and say of us that though we imagine ourselves to be friends, — I include myself with you, — we have not yet been able to find out what a friend is."

LACHES.

LACHES.

CHARACTERS.

SOCRATES.
LYSIMACHUS, *son of* ARISTIDES.
MELESIAS, *son of* THUCYDIDES.
TWO BOYS, *sons of* LYSIMACHUS *and* MELESIAS.
NICIAS, } *Athenian generals.*
LACHES,

LACHES.

178 *Lysimachus.* You have now, Nicias and Laches, seen the man who fights in armour,[1] though you do not yet know why Melesias and I urged your going with us to see him, as we did not tell you at the time. This we will now do, for we think it right to be open with you. Some there are who turn matters of this kind into ridicule and, if asked advice, will not say what they really think, but guess at the wishes of their questioner, and speak contrary to their own convictions. You, however, we believe capable not only of forming an opinion, but, having formed it, of stating it frankly; and so we have taken you into our counsel touching that which we are about to 179 unfold. Well, what I have been so long in getting at is this. Here are our two sons: this one, who belongs to Melesias, is named after his grandfather Thucydides; the other one, who is mine, likewise bears the name of his grandfather and of my father, — Aristides we call him.[2] Now we are determined to give them the best possible care, not letting them when they are only half grown do exactly as they please, after the fashion of many parents, but beginning at once to do the best we possibly can for them.

Knowing, therefore, that you too have sons, we supposed that you, if any one, would have taken thought what treatment would most improve them; and if you have not paid much attention to this, we will remind you that it is a duty not to be neglected, and will exhort you to make common cause with us in the care of our sons.

And you must hear, Nicias and Laches, what brought this to our minds, though the tale be somewhat long. We two, Melissus and I, live together, and our sons with us. Now, as I said in the beginning, we will be open with you. Of our fathers we have each of us many and noble deeds to relate to the lads, — deeds done in war and in peace, in managing the affairs of the allies, as well as of this city, — but of our own deeds neither of us has a word to say. This is of course humiliating, and we blame our fathers for having let us run wild when we were young, while they themselves were attending to the interests of others. And these things we hold up as a warning to our boys, telling them that if they disobey us and are indifferent to their own improvement their lives will be inglorious; while if they apply themselves they will doubtless become worthy of the names they bear. And as they, on their part, promise to obey, we are now considering what they must study or practise, if they would become men of worth. Now some one suggested to us this art, saying what a fine thing it is for a youth to learn how

to fight in armour, and praising the man whose exhibition you have seen, and advising us to see it for ourselves. Accordingly we thought it our duty to go to see the show, taking you with us as spectators and at the same time, if you are willing, as advisers and partners in the
180 care of our sons. This is what we wished to impart to you. It is for you now to advise us whether in your opinion the art is one to be studied or not, and whether there is any other pursuit or branch of knowledge that you could recommend for a young man, and to say, moreover, what you will do in regard to joining us.

Nicias. For my part, Lysimachus and Melesias, I commend your intention and am ready to join you; and so I think is Laches here.

Laches. You are right, Nicias, in so thinking. What Lysimachus has said about his own father and the father of Melesias is quite true, it seems to me, not only of them, but of ourselves and all who have to do with public affairs,—they treat their children and their other private concerns very nearly as he says, setting them aside and making them of no account. You are quite right, Lysimachus, in what you say. But I wonder that you summon us to advise with you about the lads' education, and not rather Socrates; for in the first place he is of your own deme, and then besides he is forever haunting places where may be found such high thinking or noble living as you are in search of for your lads.

Lys. What do you mean, Laches? Has our friend Socrates turned his attention to any of these matters?

Lach. Certainly he has, Lysimachus.

Nic. I, no less than Laches, can testify to that, for he lately recommended to me a man as teacher of music for my boys, — Damon, the pupil of Agathocles,[3] — who is not only the most accomplished of men in music, but is in all other respects a most suitable person to consort with boys of my son's age.

Lys. Those who are of my time of life, friends Socrates, Nicias, and Laches, do not know young men at all well, because our age keeps us for the most part at home. But if you, son of Sophroniscus, have any good advice to offer this fellow-demesman of yours, pray do so. This is but right, since you are my friend by right of descent from your father. He and I were always comrades and friends, and up to the day of his death there was never any difference between us. And I recollect hearing these boys say something on the subject only lately. When they are talking together at home, they are constantly bringing up the name of Socrates, and lauding him extravagantly. Tell me, boys, is this the Socrates whom you are all the time talking about?

Boy. Yes, father, the very same.

Lys. You have done well, Socrates, by Hera, in reflecting such credit upon that best of men, your father, and above all in reviving the family bonds between us.

Lach. Yes, indeed, Lysimachus, you had better not let him go.; for I remember seeing him on another occasion when he reflected credit not only upon his father, but upon his fatherland. In the flight from Delium, he and I made the retreat together; and I can only say that if others had shown themselves such as he, our city would have held her own and not at that time suffered such loss.[4]

Lys. This is high praise, Socrates, which you are receiving from men worthy of trust in the matters whereof they speak. Rest assured that I rejoice to hear of your being held in esteem, and count me one of your warmest well-wishers. You ought long ago to have looked upon us as kinsmen and come constantly to our house, as was fitting; and, now that we have revived acquaintance, you must, I insist, from this day forward be on intimate terms with us and with these youths, that our friendship may thus be preserved. We shall rely upon you then to do your part, and shall not fail to keep you in mind of it. But what do you say to what we were speaking about? What think you? Is it useful or is it not for our boys to learn fighting in armour?

Soc. Well, of course, Lysimachus, I will, as best I can, advise you and do all else that you bid. But it seems to me fairer, seeing that I am younger and less experienced than the others, to let me first hear what they have to say and to learn of them, and then if anything contrary to what has been said occurs to me I can inform you of it, and convince you and the others of its truth. So why, Nicias, should not one of you speak first?

[181 D.–187 D. Nicias, as champion of the art in question, sets forth its various advantages, but is met by the objection, from Laches, that the Lacedaemonians, although greatest in matters of war, have never known this art:

183 A. "And even," Laches asserts, "if they themselves had not known it, surely the teachers of the art must have been aware that the Lacedaemonians pay more attention than all the rest of the Hellenes to matters of the kind, and that any one who had gained their esteem would be sure to command the highest price elsewhere, as is the case with any tragic poet who has gained the esteem of our own people. Insomuch that any one who thinks he can write a fine tragedy does not go about exhibiting in the other cities of Attica, but hurries straight here, as a matter of course, and exhibits to us.[5] But I observe that these fighters in armour, on the contrary, regard Lacedaemon as a holy place where one may not set foot even on tiptoe; and so, keeping on the outer edge of the circle, they prefer to exhibit anywhere else, and especially to those

who by their own confession are inferior to others in matters relating to war. . . . Neither has any one of the men who practise this art ever distinguished himself in war. . . . For instance, this very Stesilaus, whom you and I have seen exhibiting to such a crowd and talking so boastfully about himself, I saw upon another occasion give in good earnest a far finer exhibition of himself, though an involuntary one.[6] He was serving on board a ship which had attacked a merchantman, and was fighting with a kind of scythe-spear, a weapon as peculiar as he himself was peculiar among men. It is not worth while to speak of the man himself, but only of what befell this same amusing invention of the scythe-spear. In fighting, he got it entangled in the rigging of the other ship, and there it stuck fast. Stesilaus tugged at it, hoping to get it free, but without success. Meanwhile the ships were slipping asunder. For a time he ran along his own ship, holding on to his spear the while; but, as the other ship passed by, drawing him and his spear after it, he let the spear slide through his hands till at last he was holding on only by the tip end. Then there arose great laughter and clapping of hands from those in the merchantman, at the figure he cut; and when some one threw a stone which fell at his feet on the deck, and he let go the spear, even those on his own trireme could no longer keep back their laughter at the sight of that scythe-spear swinging mid-air from the merchantman." The lesson drawn is that "no one, except he be of surpassing valour, can escape being ridiculous if he boasts of possessing the art in question."

186 A. Socrates, on being asked for his opinion declares that where the education of children, " the greatest of our possessions," is in question, our first care should be to secure the advice of one who has had good teachers and is himself skilled in the care of the soul. "As for me," he adds, "I am the first to admit that I have never had a teacher in these matters, though from my youth up I have longed for one. But I have not the means to give the Sophists their hire,[7] and they alone proclaim themselves able to turn me out a perfect man; while as to discovering the art for myself, I am as yet incapable of it." . . .

Socrates now suggests that Nicias and Laches, who add to the advantages of wealth that of riper years, be asked to give proof of their qualifications. Lysimachus accordingly requests that these two will, with the help of Socrates, examine the subject in question, and answer whatever Melesias may think proper to ask.]

187 D. *Nic.* You do of a truth, Lysimachus, appear to know Socrates only through his father, and to have had no acquaintance with the man himself, unless perhaps you may have met him amongst your fellow-demesmen when as a child

he was accompanying his father to a temple or to some other gathering of the people.[8] But that you have not come across him since he has grown older is very plain.

Lys. Why, Nicias, what do you mean?

Nic. You do not seem aware that if any one comes into close contact with Socrates and is drawn into a conversation with him, no matter what subject is first started, the man keeps leading him about in argument until he falls into the pitfall, and has to give an account of himself, and of the way in which he is now living and has lived in the past; and when once he has him there, Socrates will not let him out until he has put him to a full and thorough test in all these matters.[9] Now I, for my part, am used to him, and know that this must be suffered at his hands; and I know, moreover, that I myself shall suffer it. But it delights me, Lysimachus, to be in his company, and I deem it no evil thing to be called to account for whatever we have done or are now doing that is not right. Rather is a man in this way compelled to use greater zeal for the time to come, if only he does not shun the lesson, but, with Solon, desires to learn so long as he has life, and does not imagine that old age brings sense of itself.[10] To me it is far from an unusual or even an unpleasant thing to be cross-examined by Socrates; and I knew some time back that, when he was present, the talk would not be confined to youths but would be extended to ourselves. As I say, then, so far as I am concerned, there is nothing to prevent his talking to us just as he likes. But see how Laches feels about it.

Lach. My feeling about discussions, Nicias, is simple, or rather not simple, but two-sided. To one and the same person, indeed, I might appear in the light of a lover and at the same time a hater of discourse. For when I hear a man speaking of virtue or any form of wisdom, if he be a true man and worthy of the words he utters, I rejoice exceedingly to see that speaker and words are in accord and harmonize one with the other; and such a man I deem to be a true musician, for he is attuned to the sweetest harmony, — not that of the lute or any instrument for pastime, but to that of true living, — his life itself a symphony wherein words are attuned to deeds. No Ionian mode is this, nor yet a Phrygian, nor a Lydian, but the pure Dorian, the only truly Greek harmony.[11] When such a man speaks I rejoice, and I appear a lover of discourse, so eagerly do I receive his words. But one who is of opposite character is a vexation to me, and all the more the better I think he speaks; and then, on the contrary, I am taken for a hater of discourse. With the words of Socrates I am not familiar; but of his deeds I have had, as you know, experience in the past, and, by these, I know him worthy to express freely the noblest thoughts. If this, then, is the case, I am at one with him; and I would gladly be questioned by such a man as he, and not ill-pleased to learn of him. Nay, I am of the same mind with Solon save in one particular. As I grow old, my desire is to learn, indeed, many things, but only of good men. Let him, then, grant me this, — a teacher who is himself good, that I may appear no reluctant or unapt scholar. But as to whether the teacher is younger than myself, or whether he has not as yet attained celebrity or anything of that kind, I care nothing at all. And so, Socrates, I would inform you, that you may instruct me and cross-examine me just as you please, and in your turn learn of me all that I know. Such is my feeling toward you ever since the day when you met danger at my side, and gave that proof of valour which is the true one for a man to give. Say, then, whatever you please, and do not take our respective ages into account.

Soc. I cannot, apparently, accuse either of you of not being ready to consult and investigate with me.

Lys. But it is a subject, Socrates, that concerns us both, for I count you as one of ourselves. Consider then in my stead what, for our boys' sake, we ought to learn of these men, and talk and advise with them. For already, by reason of my age, I forget much of what I have in mind to ask; and if other talk comes in between, I cannot remember very well what I may have heard. Do you, therefore, talk over and discuss among yourselves the subjects we have started. I will listen, and afterward Melesias and I will do whatever you think best.

[189 D.-200. As the object of the present inquiry is to ascertain how virtue may be imparted, the first step is to learn its true nature by attempting the definition of some one part, — as, for instance, courage.

190 E. Of this Laches confidently asserts that "it is not hard to define. If a man remains at his post and repels the enemy, and does not flee before them, he surely is a man of courage."

But here, Socrates objects, we have but an imperfect illustration, since some modes of warfare, such as the Scythian, consist solely in retreat. What, then, he asks, is that power or quality which makes a man brave not only in war and dangers of the sea, in disease and poverty, pains and fears, but which enables him to fight also against desires and pleasures, both at his post and in the retreat?

192 E. "Endurance of the soul," is the answer.

But this too is shown to be not universally applicable, since there may be such a thing as foolish endurance.

194 "Let us, however," Socrates urges, "stand by our search and endure to the end, lest courage laugh us to scorn for not making a courageous search; for it is quite possible

that courage may turn out to be the same as endurance."

To this Laches replies: "I am quite prepared, Socrates, not to give up; for although I am unaccustomed to this kind of argument, a certain spirit of dissatisfaction has got hold of me as to what has been said, and I am really vexed at not being able to express what is in my mind. I seem to have an idea of what courage is; but it has, I know not how, slipped away from me, so that I cannot get hold of the right word or say what it is."

"But must not the good huntsman, my friend," asks Socrates, "follow up his prey, and relax no effort?"

"By all means," is the answer.

"Well, should you like to summon Nicias to the chase, and see if he is better equipped than we are?"

"I should like it," Laches replies. "Why not do so?"

"Come then, Nicias," Socrates urges, " and, if you have the strength, rescue these your friends who are tempest-tossed in a sea of argument and sore perplexed. You see, indeed, in what straits we are. If you will tell us what you take courage to be, you will put an end to these perplexities of ours and at the same time confirm your own opinions."

Nicias, recalling an old saying of Socrates, that "Courage is a kind of wisdom," now ventures to

195 define it as "the knowledge of what is or is not to be feared."

"What strange things he is saying, Socrates!" Laches remarks.

"How, Laches, do you mean?"

"How? Why, surely, knowledge is different from courage!"

"Nicias says not."

"But that is not true, by Zeus!" Laches exclaims; "there is just where he talks nonsense."

"Shall we not then," Socrates suggests, "instruct rather than abuse him?"

"Nay, Socrates," cries Nicias; "I believe what Laches wants is to make out that I am talking nonsense, because he himself is proved to have talked it."

"I shall most certainly try to make this out, Nicias," Laches admits, "for it is nonsense you are talking."

The objection which Laches brings is that physicians and other professional men are not a whit more courageous for all their knowledge.

"What do you think, Nicias," Socrates asks, "of what Laches says? There does seem to be something in it."

"Yes," Nicias replies, "something in it there is, but it is not true." And he proceeds to show that the physician's knowledge extends only to the disease, not to its ultimate effect upon his patients, so that he cannot judge whether it is better for them to die or to get well. Not even the soothsayer can decide this, nor indeed can any one else, save he who knows thoroughly what is or is not to be feared; and he alone is courageous.

196 A. At this Laches, waxing wroth, exclaims: "I do not understand, Socrates, what he means to say, unless it be that the courageous man is a god.[12] He seems unwilling frankly to acknowledge that what he says amounts to nothing, but turns and twists about, in order to conceal that he is in a quandary. If you and I had wished to avoid the appearance of contradicting ourselves, we too might have twisted about in the same way. Now, had we been arguing in a court of law, there might have been some sense in such behaviour; but why in such a meeting as this should any one trick himself out to no purpose with empty words?"

"I do not think one ought, Laches," Socrates rejoins. "But let us see; perhaps Nicias is not merely talking for argument's sake, and does mean something by what he says. Let us question him more closely as to what he has in mind, and if there seems to be anything in it, let us agree with him; if not, let us enlighten him."

"Very well, Socrates," is the reply. "If you wish to question him, do so. For my part, I have had enough of questioning."

"No trouble about that, for the same questioning will do for you and for me." According to the definition of Nicias, Socrates continues, courage would appear to be an attribute which belongs to no animal, not even to a lion or a bull.

197 In great delight Laches exclaims: "Aye, by the gods, Socrates; you are right there."

Nothing daunted, Nicias asks: "Do you suppose that children, who by reason of their ignorance are afraid of nothing, can be called courageous? Nay, to me it seems that fearlessness and courage are not at all the same thing. Few, I imagine, possess courage together with forethought; while foolhardiness, recklessness, and fearlessness are the share of many, men and women and children and beasts alike. Hence what you and many others call courage I call foolhardiness; only wise actions do I count as courageous."

"See, Socrates," Laches cries, "how well this fellow tricks out his argument, at least in his own opinion! Those whom all unite in calling courageous he undertakes to defraud of this honour."

"Not I, Laches," Nicias replies, "never fear; you I do call wise, and Lamachus too,—that is, if you are courageous,—and a great many other Athenians besides."

"I might answer; but I shall say nothing, that you may not taunt me with being a true Aexonian." [18]

"Answer nothing at all, Laches," Socrates interposes; "for you have not observed, I imagine, that he has got this wisdom of his from our friend Damon; and Damon is forever with Prodicus, who of all the Sophists seems to me best at drawing word-distinctions of this kind."

"And far more fitting it is, Socrates," Laches replies, "for a Sophist to invent subtleties of this kind, than for a man whom the State deems worthy to stand at its head."

"Nevertheless, my best of friends, it is most fitting that he to whom the greatest concerns are confided should have the greatest share of wisdom; and it seems to me quite worth while to examine what Nicias was thinking of in defining courage as he did."

"Then examine for yourself, Socrates," is the somewhat surly reply.

"That is just what I intend doing, my excellent friend;" and so, with the warning that Laches must stand ready to lend his aid, Socrates proceeds to show that if courage included the knowledge ascribed to it by Nicias, it would embrace not merely a part of virtue, but the whole of it.

Laches now taunts Nicias with the failure of his attempt to define courage:]

Lach. For my part, my dear Nicias, I certainly thought you were going to make the discovery, so contemptuous were you when I was answering Socrates. Great indeed, I may say, was my hope that you would find it out by the help of Damon's wisdom.

Nic. It is clever of you, Laches, to take no

200

further account of having just shown yourself ignorant in regard to courage, but to be only on the lookout whether I also am in the same case; and it is, I suppose, a matter of indifference to you that you and I are equally ignorant of what a man of any pretensions ought to know. You have acted, it seems to me, in a truly human fashion, looking not to yourself but to others. It strikes me, however, that I have now said quite enough on the subject in question; and if there remains anything not sufficiently explained, this may be remedied later with the help of others, and especially of Damon, whom you imagine yourself to have laughed down, although you have never even seen him. And when I am sure of my own ground, I will instruct you also without grudging, for you seem to me in great need of instruction.

Lach. How wise you are, Nicias, to be sure! But all the same, when it comes to the education of these lads, I advise my friend Lysimachus here and Melesias, to dismiss you and me, but, as I said before, not to let our friend Socrates go. If my children were of a proper age, that is what I should do.

Nic. Yes, I agree to that, and advise them to seek no further, if Socrates is willing to take charge of the lads. Indeed I would most gladly confide my Niceratus [14] to him, if he would only consent; but whenever I bring the matter up to him he is sure to recommend some one else, and is not willing to do anything himself. But you might see, Lysimachus, if he will perhaps listen to you more readily.

Lys. That would be only fair of him, Nicias, for I would do for him what I would not for many others. What say you then, Socrates? Will you comply with our wishes and unite to help these lads become as good as possible?

Soc. It would be a dreadful thing, Lysimachus, not to be willing to help any one to become better. And so, if our late conversation had proved that I knew and these two did not, it would be right to urge me most strongly to undertake the duty; but as it is, we are all in the same perplexity. Why then should any one of us be chosen before the other? To my mind, no one deserves the preference. This being the state of the case, consider whether the advice I am about to give you is good. I declare to you, my friends, — and let no one report it outside, — that it behooves us all earnestly to seek out the best teacher we can get, for ourselves first of all, — for we need him, — and then for the lads, sparing neither money nor anything else. But to remain in our present condition I cannot advise. And if any one makes fun of us because we think it right at our age to go to school, we must, I think, shield ourselves behind Homer, who says that "shame ill becomes a beggar-man." And so, paying no heed to any one's remarks, we will make our own education and that of the lads our common care.

Lys. What you say, Socrates, pleases me. And I desire that as I am the eldest, so I may also be the most eager to learn with these boys. Pray then do me this favour. Come without fail to my house to-morrow early, that we may take counsel together about these matters. But for the present we must bring our interview to a close.

Soc. I will do as you wish, Lysimachus, and to-morrow, God willing, I will come.

EUTHYDEMUS.

EUTHYDEMUS.

CHARACTERS.

SOCRATES, *who narrates to his friend* CRITO *a conversation in which the following persons take part:—*

EUTHYDEMUS,
DIONYSODORUS, } *two brothers, Sophists.*
CLEINIAS, *son of* AXIOCHUS, *a young Athenian.*
CTESIPPUS *of Paeania, an admirer of* CLEINIAS.

The scene is laid in the Lyceum.

EUTHYDEMUS.

271 *Crito.* Who was it, Socrates, whom you were talking with yesterday in the Lyceum? There was such a crowd around you that, although I tried to get near enough to listen, I could not make out anything distinctly. By bending over, however, I could look down upon you, and it seemed to me that it was a stranger you were talking with. Who was he?

Socrates. Which one are you asking about, Crito? There were two of them.

Cri. The man I mean was seated next but one from you on the right; between you was the young son of Axiochus,[1] who seems to me, Socrates, to have grown wonderfully, and to be not far from the age of our own Critobulus. But while he is slight in build, this lad is well developed and of fine presence.

Soc. Euthydemus is the man you mean, Crito; and the one seated on my left was his brother Dionysodorus, who also took part in the conversation.[2]

Cri. I do not know either of them, Socrates. They are, I suppose, some more new Sophists. Where do they come from, and what branch of wisdom do they profess?

Soc. By descent they are from hereabouts, from Chios, I believe, whence they removed to Thurii;[3] but they were banished from there, and have been living a number of years now in these parts. As for their wisdom which you were asking about, it is marvellous, Crito, — they are simply all-wise. For my part, I never knew till now what the pancratiasts really were. These two are ready for every kind of contest, — and that not after the fashion of the Acarnanians, the pancratiast brothers, who knew how to fight only with the body. In the first place, they are most skilful with the body, and have a superior mode of fighting, by which they overcome all others; for they are complete masters of the art of fighting in armour, and able, moreover, to impart it to any one else who will pay them.[4] And secondly, they are excellent in controversies of law; contending themselves, and teaching others to speak and to compose speeches such as are suitable for courts of justice. Up to this time they have excelled in these branches alone, but now they have put the finishing touch to their pancratiastic art. The one kind of combat which they had hitherto left untried they have now brought to such perfection that no one is able even to stand against them, so formidable have they become in the art of word-fighting and refuting whatever statement is made, whether it happens to be true or false. Really, Crito, I have a mind to put myself into the hands of these men; for they promise that in a short time they will make any one whomsoever skilful in these matters.

Cri. Why, Socrates! Are you not afraid that at your time of life you are too old for that?

Soc. Not in the least, Crito. I have ample reason and encouragement for not fearing it. For they themselves were, one might say, old men when they first took up this art of disputation which I covet. Why, only last year, or the year before, they had not yet knowledge of it! But one thing I do fear, — that I may bring contempt upon these strangers, just as I do upon Connus, the son of Metrobius the cithara-player, who is still giving me lessons upon the cithara. For when the boys, my fellow-pupils, see me there, they make fun of me and dub Connus "old man's teacher." Now I trust that no one will insult these two strangers in this way, but I dare say they may fear it for themselves, and be unwilling to receive me. And therefore, Crito, as I then persuaded certain old men to go with me as fellow-pupils, so I shall try to prevail upon others now. And you, — why should not you make one of us? We might bring your sons with us as a bait; for in the desire to get hold of them, they will, I know, instruct us also.

Cri. There can be no objection, Socrates, I am sure, if you wish it. But first, pray, give me some account of the men's art, that I may know what it is we are to learn of them.

Soc. You shall hear without delay. I certainly could not plead inattention as an excuse, for I did attend most carefully; and as I remember what they said, I shall endeavour to give you the whole story from the beginning.

By the favour doubtless, of some god, I happened to be seated alone in the robing-room just where you saw me, and I had in mind to get up and go away, when, in the very act of rising,[5] there came to me the accustomed divine sign. Accordingly I sat down again, and a little while after came in these two, Euthydemus and Dionysodorus, and with them a number of others, — their pupils I suppose they were. On entering, they began to pace around the covered course. Hardly, however, had they taken two or three turns when Cleinias came in, who, as you rightly observe, is vastly improved; and in his train a great number of admirers, — amongst them Ctesippus the Paeanian,[6] a young man of good natural parts, but with the impetuosity of his years. Cleinias, as he entered, seeing me seated by myself, crossed over and sat down at my right, just where you say he was. When Dionysodorus and Euthydemus saw him there, I observed — for I was watching them closely — that they at first stopped still and talked together, casting every now and then a glance at us. Then they drew near; and one of them, Euthydemus, took a seat next the youth, the other a seat next me on the left, while the rest found places for themselves just as it chanced. As I had not seen them for some time, I saluted them, and then, turning to Cleinias, —

"You must know, Cleinias," I said, "that these two men, Euthydemus and Dionysodorus, are skilled in matters not of trifling, but of most serious import. They understand everything that has to do with war; all that a man who is to be a leader need know about the disposition and conduct of armies, and all about fighting in armour. And they can, moreover, make him capable of defending himself in the courts of justice, if any one does him an injury."

These words drew upon me their contempt. Glancing at each other they burst out laughing, and Euthydemus said, —

"We no longer care for that kind of thing, Socrates; we only use it incidentally."

Wondering at this, I said, —

"Grand, indeed, must be your chief pursuit, if such as this is only incidental! In the name of the gods, then, tell me what is this grand pursuit of yours?"

"Virtue, Socrates," he replied; "and this we believe ourselves capable of imparting more speedily and effectually than any other man."[7]

"Oh, Zeus!" I exclaimed, "what a wonderful thing is this! Where did you discover such a treasure? As I said just now, I have always supposed the art you had mastered was that of fighting in armour; and this is what I have said of you, remembering that when you first stayed here it was what you professed. But if you really possess this other knowledge, then take pity on me. I call upon you even as upon gods, and entreat your forgiveness for what I have said of you heretofore. But see to it, Euthydemus and Dionysodorus, that you are saying what is true, for your promise is so great that there is no wonder it is questioned."

"You may rest assured, Socrates," they answered, "that all is as we have said."

"Then I count you far happier with this possession of yours than is the great King with his kingdom. But tell me, do you intend to exhibit this knowledge, or what do you intend to do?"

"Why this, Socrates, is the very reason we are here, — to exhibit it, and to impart it, if any one wishes to learn of us."

"Well, I give you my word that all who do not possess it will wish to do so, myself to begin with, then Cleinias here, and beside us, Ctesippus and all the rest of the company."

Thus I spoke, pointing to the admirers of Cleinias, who by this time were gathered around us. Now Ctesippus, as it chanced, had been seated at some distance from Cleinias, so that whenever in talking with me Euthydemus happened to lean forward, Cleinias, who was placed between us two, was hidden from the sight of Ctesippus.

He, therefore, being anxious to see his favourite and to hear at the same time, was the first to jump up and place himself directly opposite us; on seeing which, the others also gathered around us,— the admirers of Cleinias, and the followers of Euthydemus and Dionysodorus as well. And these it was whom I pointed out to Euthydemus, when I said that they were all ready to be instructed. To this Ctesippus and the others gave eager assent, all with one voice urging them to show what their art could do.

Then I said, —

"I hope, on every account, Euthydemus and Dionysodorus, that you will do this company and myself the favour of giving us an exhibition. To do it in full would of course be no slight task; but at least tell me whether you would be able to make him alone a virtuous man who already believes it is his duty to learn of you, or him also who is not yet convinced of this, because he disbelieves the whole thing,— either that virtue can be taught or that you are teachers of it. Tell me, is it the business of this particular art or of some other, to convince one of this mind that virtue may be taught, and that you are the men from whom it may best be learned?"

"Certainly, Socrates," Dionysodorus replied, "it is the business of this particular art."

"So then, Dionysodorus," said I, "you two, of
275 all living men, can best turn others toward philosophy and the cultivation of virtue?"

"Yes, Socrates; at least we ourselves think so."

"Pray, then," said I, "put off to another time your exhibition for other cases, and show us now what you can do for this particular one. Convince this lad here that it is his duty to follow philosophy and cultivate virtue, and you will be doing a favour to me and all the others For the fact in regard to this youth is that we are most anxious, I and all the rest of us, to have him grow up the best of men. He is the son of Axiochus, and thus grandson of Alcibiades the elder and own cousin to the present Alcibiades, — Cleinias is his name. He is young still, and we are fearful, as we may well be considering his age, lest some one get ahead of us, and, by turning his mind to some other pursuit, bring about his ruin; so that you have come most opportunely. Pray, then, if you have no objection, make trial of the boy, and let your conversation be held before us."

After I had spoken pretty nearly these words, Euthydemus began in a brisk and even confident way.

"Of course, Socrates," said he, "we have no objection, if only the young man himself is willing to answer."

"Oh, as to that," I replied, "he is well accustomed to it. These friends of his are in the habit of coming and asking him all manner of questions, and arguing with him; so that he is fairly confident about answering."

And now, Crito, how shall I fitly describe to you what followed? It is no light task to take up in detail a wisdom which is, so to speak, infinite. It behooves me, even as the poets, to begin my narration by invoking Memory and the Muses. Euthydemus, so far as I can recollect, began in some such way as this, —

"To what class of men, Cleinias, do they belong who learn, — to the wise or the ignorant?"

Taken aback by the vastness of the question, the young fellow blushed and looked at me; and I, perceiving that he was in trouble, —

"Take heart, Cleinias," I said, "and answer boldly just which you think, for in that way you will probably derive the greatest benefit."

Hereupon Dionysodorus, his face wearing a broad smile, bent over and said softly in my ear, —

"I tell you beforehand, Socrates, and do you mark my words, that whatever the boy answers he is sure to be refuted."

While he was speaking, Cleinias was giving his answer, so that I did not have a chance to bid the lad be on his guard, and he answered that they who learn are the wise; whereupon Euthydemus asked, —

"Are there such people as teachers, or are there not?"

He assented.

"And teachers are the teachers of those who learn, are they not, just as the cithara-player and the writing-master were your teachers and those of other boys, and you their pupils?"

"Yes," he replied.

"And at the time you were learning, you did not yet know the things you were learning, did you?"

"No," he said.

"But were you wise, if you did not know them?"

"Of course not," he said.

"Then if not wise, you were ignorant?"

"Very ignorant."

"So then, learning what you did not know, you were ignorant when you were learning."

The lad nodded assent.

"Thus, Cleinias, it is the ignorant who learn, not the wise, as you suppose."[8]

Hardly had he spoken thus, when, for all the world like a chorus which has had its cue from the trainer, the followers of Euthydemus and Dionysodorus began with one accord to laugh and cheer; and before the lad had fully recovered his breath, Dionysodorus took up the argument.

"Tell me, Cleinias," he said, "when the reading-master used to dictate to you, which of the boys would learn the dictation, — the wise or the ignorant?"

"The wise," Cleinias answered.

"Then it is the wise who learn, not the ignorant, and the answer you gave Euthydemus just now is not correct."

Then again there was great laughter and applause from the two men's admirers, who were enraptured at their cleverness, while the rest of us, amazed, held our peace. Euthydemus, however, perceiving our amazement and anxious to win yet more admiration, did not let the lad go but went on questioning him, and, like some nimble dancer, gave the question a double turn upon itself and asked, —

"What is it that learners learn, — what they know or what they do not know?"

Here Dionysodorus again whispered softly to me, —

"This, Socrates, is just such another question as the one before."

"Heavens!" I exclaimed; "and your last question seemed so brilliant."

"All that we ask, Socrates," he rejoined, "are of the same sort, admitting of no possible escape."

"This is the reason, I suppose," said I, "that you have such a reputation among your followers."

In the mean time Cleinias had answered that learners learn what they do not know, and Euthydemus was putting him through the same kind of questioning as before.

"Tell me this," he said. "You know your letters, do you not?"

"Yes," he answered.

"All of them, I suppose?"

He admitted that he did.

"And when any one dictates, no matter what it be, does he not dictate letters?"

He admitted it.

"But if you know them all, he is dictating what you already knew, is he not?"

This too he admitted.

"How now?" said he; "surely it is not you who learn what is dictated, but he who does not know letters."

"Not so," he answered; "it is I who learn."

"But since you know all the letters, you are only learning what you know."

He confessed that it was so.

"Therefore," said he, "you have not answered correctly."

Hardly had Euthydemus thus spoken, when Dionysodorus, taking up the argument as if it were a ball, aimed another throw at the lad, and said, —

"Euthydemus is playing a trick upon you, Cleinias. Tell me this: To learn is to acquire knowledge of whatever one learns, is it not?"

Cleinias assented.

"And what is to know, but already to have knowledge?"

He assented.

"Or not to know, but not yet to have knowledge?"

He agreed to that.

"And are they who acquire anything those who have it already, or those who do not have it?"

"Those who do not have it."

"But have you not admitted that they who do not know belong to those who as yet do not have?"

He nodded assent.

"And they who learn belong to those who acquire, not to those who already have?"

This he acknowledged.

"And so, Cleinias, it is they that do not know who learn, not they that know."

And now for the third time Euthydemus was about to bear down upon the lad for another bout, when, perceiving that the young fellow was out of his depth, and wishing to let him rest awhile and not get disheartened, I said encouragingly, —

"You must not be surprised, Cleinias, if this talk seems to you strange. Very likely you do not perceive that these strangers are doing to you just what is done in the initiation rites of the Corybantes,[9] at the enthronement of him whom they are about to initiate. On that occasion there is dancing and frolicking, as you must know, if you have ever been initiated. And so now these two are merely dancing, and, as it were, gambolling playfully about you, by way of prelude to your initiation."

[277 E.–282 D. Socrates now shows that confusion has arisen from using the word "learning," once in its sense of the acquisition of knowledge, and again in the sense of knowledge already acquired. The horse-play of the brothers is compared to the action of one who, when a man is about to seat himself, suddenly withdraws the chair from under him and laughs in glee to see him tumble over backward. Assuming that they have now had their fill of this kind of amusement, he proceeds, with many apologies for his own lack of skill, to set them an example of serious questioning by means of which the following conclusions are reached.

Happiness, the object of all men's desire, comes from the possession of good things, whether external gifts or moral qualities, such as courage, justice, and the like. But since only by right use do these possessions become a good and not an evil fortune, wisdom, which alone ensures their right use, must prove the truest blessing, as ignorance is in reality the only evil. Cleinias, on declaring his belief that wisdom does not come unsought, but must be acquired, is earnestly exhorted by Socrates to apply himself to the quest of it, and replies with like earnestness:]

"Indeed, Socrates, I will do my best."
And I, delighted to hear this, —
"Here, Dionysodorus and Euthydemus," I said, "is my example of what I think an exhortation

ought to be, though unskilful, I dare say, and expressed laboriously with many words. And now let one of you, whichever pleases, go over the same ground in a scientific manner; or if you do not care for this, begin where I left off and show the lad in due sequence whether he must needs acquire every kind of knowledge, or whether there is but one kind which a man need acquire in order to be good and happy, and what that is. For, as I said in the beginning, we have it much at heart that the lad should become a wise and a good man."

283   Thus, Crito, did I speak, and, all eagerness to know what was to follow, I watched to see how they would take hold of the subject, and whence start in their exhortations to the practice of wisdom and virtue. The elder of the two, Dionysodorus, had the first word; and upon him we all fixed our gaze, expecting to hear something wonderful. And this, in fact, was our good fortune, for a wonderful discourse it certainly was, Crito, which the man began, and one well worth your hearing, so stimulating was it to the pursuit of virtue.

"Tell me, Socrates," he began, "you and the rest who say that you want this youth to become a wise man,—do you speak in jest, or do you really wish it in good earnest?"

From this I inferred that they had all along supposed us to be in jest when we urged them to converse with the lad, and that this was why they too had jested and had not treated it seriously. With this thought I said, in a still more decided way, that we were exceedingly in earnest. Thereupon Dionysodorus, —

"Look to it, Socrates," he said, "that you do not come to deny what you now assert."

"I have looked to it," I said, "and shall never deny it."

"Well, what is it you say?" he asked, "that you wish him to become wise?"

"That I do."

"Very well; which is Cleinias now, wise or not?"

"He himself says not, but then he is no braggart."

"And you," he said, "wish him to become wise, and not ignorant?"

We owned that we did.

"Then that which he is not you wish him to become, and to be no longer that which he is now?"

I was disconcerted at this; and he, taking advantage of my discomfiture, added, —

"In wishing him to be no longer that which he is now, what are you wishing but his destruction? Fine friends and admirers, indeed, are those who would do everything to bring their favourite to destruction!"

At this, Ctesippus, moved to anger on his favourite's account, cried out, —

"Stranger of Thurii, if it were not too ill-bred to speak thus, I should say, 'On your head be the evil!'[10] What are you thinking of in falsely accusing me and the others of a thing which it seems to me impious even to utter; namely, that I could wish to bring him to destruction?"

[283 E.–284 E. Euthydemus replies to this sally by denying the possibility of speaking falsely. That which has no existence, he argues, is not, and cannot therefore be spoken of. But that which has existence is; and he who says what is, speaks the truth.

Still further incensed by this specious reasoning, Ctesippus aims a pointed thrust at Dionysodorus, who forthwith exclaims:]

"You insult me, Ctesippus, you insult me!"

"Not I, by Zeus!" he answered. "On the contrary, I have a regard for you. I am only warning you as a friend, and endeavouring to persuade you never again in my presence to say so ill-mannered a thing as that I wish to ruin those whom I hold most dear."

Here, thinking that they were getting too rude to one another, I began to rally Ctesippus.

"It strikes me, Ctesippus," I said, "that we ought to accept from the strangers whatever they are kind enough to give us, and not have disputes about a word. For if they know the art of so utterly destroying people as to turn them from bad and foolish men into good and sensible ones, — whether they have found out for themselves or have learned from some one else this kind of ruin and destruction matters not, — if, I say, they know how to effect this (and it is evident that they do, for they certainly spoke of their newly discovered art of making good men out of bad), why we will allow them. Let them destroy the lad for us and make him wise, and all the rest of us as well. If, however, you younger ones are afraid, then let the danger be upon my head, as if I were a Carian.[11] For being an old man, I am ready to make the venture; and so I offer myself up to this Dionysodorus, as it might be to Medea the Colchian. Let him destroy, yea, boil me, if he likes; let him, in short, do whatever he pleases, if only he turns me out a good man."

"I too, Socrates," said Ctesippus, "am ready to give myself up to the strangers, and let them flay me, if they wish, even more severely than they have done already, if only my skin may find its end, not like that of Marsyas, in a wine-bottle, but in virtue. Now Dionysodorus imagines that I am angry with him, whereas I am not angry, but only contradict things that he says against me which I do not think are right. But I must beg of you, most noble Dionysodorus, not to call contradiction insult; for insult is quite a different thing."

"Are you speaking of contradiction, Ctesippus," Dionysodorus asked, "as a real thing?"

"Of course I am," he answered; "most emphatically so. And you, Dionysodorus, do you not believe in contradiction?"

"I defy you," he said, "to prove that you ever heard one person contradict another."

"Very good," he said; "we shall soon see if I cannot show you that Ctesippus can contradict Dionysodorus."

[285 E.–290 E. In spite of this boast, the sophistry of his opponent soon reduces Ctesippus to silence. But Socrates, throwing himself into the breach, speedily proves that even the Sophist's art, "all amazing" as it is, has not taught him the art of throwing another without falling himself. By this time Ctesippus has regained his usual confidence, and exclaims:

288 B. "Wonderful talk is this of yours, men of Thurii or Chios, or wherever else you come from, and whatever you may be pleased to be called! You stop at no nonsense."

Here Socrates, fearful lest further insults should follow, calms Ctesippus by saying, —

"I tell you, Ctesippus, what I told Cleinias just now, — that you have no conception of how wonderful is the wisdom of these strangers. Till now they have been unwilling to exhibit to us in good earnest, but, after the example of Proteus the Egyptian Sophist,[12] have been casting their spells upon us. Let us therefore, after the example of Menelaus, not let the men go until they have shown us what is their real aim; for it is my belief that when they once begin in good earnest, they will reveal something of surpassing beauty. Let us, then, pray and beseech them to show this forth. And I think that I will give them once more an example of the way in which I pray them to reveal themselves to me. I will begin, then, from where I left off, and for their sakes will do my best to go through the remainder in due order, hoping so to excite their pity and compassion at the sight of my efforts and my earnestness, that they too may show themselves in earnest."

Philosophy, or the study of wisdom, has been found to be the acquisition of knowledge. What then is the special knowledge which will bring us happiness, by enabling us to use to the greatest advantage the good that is within us? Among the various arts proposed to this end is the composition of speeches. But this, as Cleinias shrewdly remarks, cannot make us happy, since "there are some speech-makers who do not know how to use the very speeches they compose." "I had certainly supposed," Socrates ironically asserts, "that knowledge, which we have been so long seeking, would have been found in this quarter. For these men, Cleinias, — the speech-makers, — whenever I come across them, appear to me excessively wise, and this very art of theirs is something lofty and inspired. And indeed, no wonder; for it is a branch of the art of enchantment, and but little inferior to it. The one consists in the charming of snakes and spiders and scorpions and other beasts and nuisances; the other in the charming and persuading of jurors and assemblies, and other bodies of men." He then proposes the general's art, which is, however, rejected by Cleinias on the ground that, instead of using and improving his spoils, the general delivers them over to the statesman just as the huntsman hands over his prey to the cook.

Amazed at the perspicacity displayed by Cleinias, Crito here interrupts the narrative by exclaiming:]

290 E. *Cri.* What are you saying, Socrates? Did the boy speak like that?

Soc. Do you not believe it, Crito?

Cri. No, by Zeus, I do not! for I am thinking that if he talked thus, he needed neither Euthydemus nor any one else to teach him.

Soc. Nay, by Zeus! perhaps I have not remembered aright, and Ctesippus was the one who said it.[13]

291 *Cri.* Ctesippus, indeed!

Soc. Well, this much, at all events, I am sure of: it was neither Euthydemus nor Dionysodorus. But may it not be, my good Crito, that some one there who was superior to them said it? For that I heard the words I am positive.

Cri. Aye, by Zeus, Socrates, some one

who I should think was their superior indeed, and very much so! But what art did you seek after this; and did you discover, or not, that which you were in search of?

Soc. Discover it, my friend? No, but we made ourselves very ridiculous. Like children in pursuit of larks, we were always fancying we had got hold of the several kinds of knowledge, and they were always slipping away from us.

[291 B.-292 E. The kingly or political art is now tried, but proves no less inadequate than the preceding ones. Here Crito a second time breaks in upon the narrative.]

Cri. By Zeus, Socrates, you do seem to have got into a quandary.

Soc. Seeing, then, Crito, that I had fallen into such extremity, I sent forth my whole voice in supplication to the strangers, calling upon them, as upon the Dioscuri,[14] to rescue us — myself and the lad as well — from the triple wave of the discussion, and to be by all means serious, and to show us in good earnest what that knowledge was through the attainment of which we might live the rest of our life in the right way.

[293 A.-303 A. The narrative is now resumed. In "haughty language," Euthydemus asks whether Socrates prefers to be instructed in this knowledge, or to have it proved that it is already his.

"Why, my good fellow," asks Socrates, "does it lie with you to do this?"

"Certainly," is the reply.

"Then by Zeus," Socrates cries, "prove that it is mine. For to a man of my years, this is far easier than getting it by study."

Thus urged, Euthydemus proceeds with the following sequence:—

"Do you know anything?

"If you do, you have knowledge.

"If you have knowledge, you know all things."

"But," Socrates remonstrates, "there are many things which I do not know."

"Then you have not knowledge, as just now you said you had."

Following out their theory that they who know one thing must know all, the two brothers now claim for themselves a knowledge not only of all the various arts, which are in turn enumerated by Ctesippus, but of all things else. 'Boldly facing every question,' we are told, 'they rushed on, like wild boars, to meet the blow.' The refusal of Socrates to follow their example and confess what he does not understand brings upon him the taunt of Euthydemus that he is "an old fogy and in his dotage."

295 D. 'Now I knew,' Socrates explains, 'that he was angry with me for exacting of him precise statements, when he had thought to catch me in a network of words. And I remembered Connus, and how angry he used to get with me

every time that I would not give in to him, and how he afterwards took less interest in me and set me down as a dullard. Therefore, as I was minded to study with him, I bethought me that I had better yield the point, for fear that he might think me a fool and not receive me as pupil. So I said, —

"'Why, of course, Euthydemus, you must do as you think best; for you, who possess the art, understand how to talk far better than I who have no knowledge of it. Pray, then, question me again from the beginning.'"

The declaration of Euthydemus that Socrates does know and has always known all things, "when a child, and when he was born, and when he was begotten, and even before his birth, and before heaven and earth were," gives rise to the inquiry where he can have learned such a thing as that good men are unjust. "Nowhere," Dionysodorus exclaims, and is forthwith reproached by his brother for "spoiling the argument." Amid the blushes of the culprit, Socrates exclaims, —

297 A. "What do you mean, Euthydemus? Do you not think that your brother, who knows all things, has spoken correctly?"

Quickly catching at this cue, —

"Am I, then," begins Dionysodorus, "the brother of Euthydemus?"

"Let that alone, my good fellow," Socrates rejoins, "at least until Euthydemus shall have taught me that I know good men to be unjust. Do not, pray, grudge my learning this."

"You are trying to run away, Socrates," is the retort, "and are refusing to answer."

"Naturally enough," Socrates admits; "for since I am inferior to either one of you singly, it were strange, indeed, if I did not run away from the two of you. I am of course a mere weakling by the side of Heracles, and even he was not able to fight both against the hydra (a she-sophist, who through her sophist art could, if one head of her argument were cut off, shoot out many more in place of it), and the crab beside,—a certain other sophist who had, I believe, just come sailing in from the sea. When therefore, with tongue and teeth, this creature began to harass him on the left side, he called for help upon his nephew Iolaus, and he indeed abundantly supplied it; whereas if Patrocles, who is my Iolaus, were to come, he would only make matters worse." [15]

This allusion to relationships leads to the following propositions: "If a man is a father, he cannot be other than a father. . . . But if he be not father to every man, he is other than a father, and cannot be yours. . . . Thus you, Socrates, are without a father." Then follow a succession of quibbles, one leading to another, not by any natural connection of ideas, but by some chance word taken advantage of by one or other of the brothers. Ctesippus, excited, as Socrates slyly conjectures, by the presence of his favourite, now begins to try his hand at the same game, and by proposing two alternatives, neither of which is tenable, succeeds in placing Euthydemus between the horns of a dilemma. Again Dionysodorus, more zealous than discreet, takes the words from his brother's mouth, exclaiming triumphantly, —

300 D. "Neither and both! There, I know well enough you can make nothing out of that answer."

'Here,' goes on the narrative, 'Ctesippus, as was his custom, burst out into a loud laugh, exclaiming,' —

"Oh, Euthydemus, this brother of yours has given two answers to one question. He is worsted and undone!"

'This delighted Cleinias, and he laughed so heartily that Ctesippus became ten times more turbulent than before.'

'I have my suspicion, however,' Socrates remarks, 'that our sly rogue of a Ctesippus had stolen this saying of his from the brothers themselves, for nowhere else among men is cleverness of this sort to be found.'

"And why, Ctesippus," Socrates now asks, "do you laugh at things so serious and beautiful?"

"Have you, then, Socrates," inquires Dionysodorus, "ever beheld a beautiful thing?"

"Indeed I have," is the reply; "and many of them too."

301 "Were they distinct from beauty, or identical with it?"

'Then, indeed,' Socrates confesses, 'did I find myself in the extreme of perplexity, and methought I had got my deserts for having ventured to speak above my breath. I said, however, that they were distinct from beauty, but that beauty was to a certain extent present with each one.'

"Then if an ox is present with you, are you an ox; and because I am present with you, are you Dionysodorus?"

After further absurdities, the proposition is finally reached and assented to by Socrates, that every man has a right to do as he pleases with his own. Whereupon Dionysodorus, 'after a long pause, during which he pretended to be pondering some grave matter,' asks, —

302 B. "Tell me, Socrates, have you an ancestral Zeus?"[16]

Socrates foresees what is coming, and after 'twisting about as if caught in a net,' replies that he has not, inasmuch as the ancestral god of Athens is Apollo, father of Ion the founder of the Ionian race. But his subsequent admission that Zeus and Athene are guardians of the phratriae is enough for Dionysodorus.

"These gods then," he cries, "are yours; and having life they are animals; and therefore, like any other of our possessions, they may be given away or sold or offered in sacrifice.]

303 A. Hereupon, Crito, struck dumb as it were by the argument, I remained speechless; but Ctesippus, advancing to my rescue, cried, —

"Bravo, Heracles! noble words are these!" With this, —

"Is Heracles bravo?" asked Dionysodorus, "or is bravo Heracles?"

"Oh, Poseidon!" exclaimed Ctesippus, "what clever talk! I give up. These two are invincible."

Then, indeed, dear Crito, there was not one of the company present who did not praise extravagantly both the argument and the men themselves, insomuch that they were nearly overpowered by the laughter and applause and merriment. For up to this time it was only the admirers of Euthydemus who had, at each hit, made such an uproar; but now the very pillars of the Lyceum seemed to join in the din, and to rejoice over the pair. For myself, I was brought to such a state that I had to confess I had never before laid eyes upon men so wise; and, quite spellbound by their wisdom, I fell to praising and congratulating them.

"Happy are you two," I said, "who are so wonderfully gifted by nature as to have wrought with such ease and speed so great a work. Your discourses, Euthydemus and Dionysodorus, are filled with beauties many and varied; but the most sublime part of all is that you care nothing for the generality of men, nor even for those who are revered and held in high esteem, but only for those who are like yourselves. For I know well that there are very few who, like you, would be satisfied with these arguments; in fact, such is the opinion which most men have of them, that they would, I am quite sure, be more ashamed to use such arguments in refuting other men, than to be themselves refuted by them. And there is this, moreover, that is kind and friendly about your arguments. When you say that there is no such thing as the beautiful, or the good, or white, or anything else of the sort, — in fact no difference at all between one thing and another, — you do, as you say, effectually stop men's mouths; and not other men's only, but your own apparently as well, which makes the thing charming and deprives your words of harshness. But, best of all, so skilful and admirable is this invention of yours that there is no one who in a very short time may not also acquire the art, as in the case of Ctesippus, who, I observed, was very soon able to imitate you off-hand. Now this feature of it, the being able to impart it quickly, is all very fine, but it is really not for your own interest to discourse in public; and, if you take my advice, you will be careful not to talk before many people, lest what they learn so quickly they give you no thanks for. Rather do you two converse together by yourselves; or if before any one else at all, let it be only before one who will pay you for it. And if you are wise, you will advise your followers also never to talk before any one else besides you and themselves. For that which is scarce, Euthydemus, is valuable; and water, for all it be, according to Pindar, the best thing, is also the cheapest.[17] But come, do not forget that you are to receive myself and Cleinias here, as your pupils."

And so, Crito, having exchanged these words and a few others, we went our ways. It is for you now to consider in what spirit you will approach these men, since they declare themselves able to teach any one who is willing to pay for it, without any exception of age or of character. But what it particularly concerns you to hear is their assertion that not even the pursuit of making money need prevent or hinder any one whomsoever from readily acquiring their wisdom.[18]

Cri. I suspect, Socrates, that, fond as I am of listening and delighted as I am to learn, I belong not to those who are like Euthydemus, but to those who you say prefer to be refuted by such arguments rather than to refute with the help of them. And though it seems ridiculous for me to be admonishing you, still I do want to tell you a thing that has come to my ears. You must know, then, that as I was walking up and down, I was joined by a man who had just come away from the group around you, — a man who thinks himself exceedingly wise, one of those clever writers of speeches for the law courts. "Well, Crito," he asked, "are you not listening to these wise men?" "No, by Zeus!" I answered; "for where I was standing I could not hear a word, on account of the crowd." "That is a pity," he said, "for it was worth hearing." "How do you mean?" "You would have heard the conversation of men who are the most skilful of our day in talk of that kind." "And what," I asked, "did they prove to you?" "What, indeed, but the kind of thing one might always hear from men who talk nonsense and bestow unworthy pains upon a worthless object!" These were about the words he used. "But still," said I, "philosophy is a pleasing thing." "Pleasing, indeed, my good fellow? It amounts to nothing at all; and 305 had you been there, you would, I think, have been very much ashamed of your friend, so preposterous was his conduct in giving himself up to men who take no thought as to what they themselves mean, and yet are sticklers for every word. And these, as I said just now, are among the best of our day! But, indeed, Crito," he added, "the thing itself, and the men who practise it, are alike contemptible and absurd."

Now, I thought to myself, Socrates, that neither this man nor any one else was right in blaming the thing itself; but your willingness to discuss with such men as these before a number of people, it seemed to me that he might justly find fault with.

[305 B.–306 D. Without noticing the reproach, Socrates explains that this man of the law courts is one of a class who regard philosophers in the light of rivals and disputants of their own rightful claim to supremacy. "Nor is it unnatural," he adds ironically, "that they should look upon themselves as wise; for to have a fair share of philosophy, and a fair amount of political knowledge as well, is a very sensible thing; that is, if they possess just enough of each to keep clear of risks and conflicts, and to reap the advantages of their own wisdom." Such a notion as this is 'more plausible than truthful,' and they who hold it are blind to the fact that to aim at a mean between two good things is to fail of attaining either, and that while they wish to stand first they are in reality only third. 'In this position, midway between philosophy and politics,' they imagine themselves to be at the head of each, whereas their knowledge is in reality of the most superficial kind.[19]]

Cri. Well, Socrates, as I am always telling you, I am in great perplexity in regard to my sons, and what I ought to do with them. The younger one, to be sure, is still small, but Critobulus is already of an age to need some one who will be of help to him. So often as I come under your influence I deem it sheer madness to have taken so much trouble on my children's account, making such a marriage as to ensure their being of noble descent, and seeking a fortune so as to enrich them,— and yet to have taken no thought for their education. But when, on the other hand, I see any of the men who profess to teach others, I am confounded, and when I come to examine them, they seem to me, one and all, to tell you the truth, perfect monstrosities; so that I know not how I can encourage the lad to follow philosophy.

Soc. My dear Crito, do you not know that in every profession there are many who are incompetent and who count for little, while they who excel are few and of priceless worth? Why, do you not regard the arts of gymnastics and money-making and public speaking and generalship as noble pursuits?

Cri. Yes, most certainly I do.

Soc. Well, but do you not see that in every one of these the greater number are absurdly deficient in their performance?

Cri. Aye, by Zeus! what you say is most true.

Soc. And would you, for this reason, shun all these pursuits yourself, and not let your son follow them?

Cri. That would not be right, Socrates.

Soc. Then do not you, Crito, act wrongly, but, dismissing the question whether they who follow philosophy are good or bad, put philosophy herself to a high and thorough test; and if she proves herself to you a poor thing, turn from her not your sons alone, but all other men beside. If on the other hand she proves herself what I myself believe that she is, then follow her rejoicing, and serve her, as the saying goes, yourself and your children.

THEAETETUS.

· THEAETETUS.

CHARACTERS.

EUCLID,
TERPSION, } *whose conversation leads to a reading of the dialogue.*

SOCRATES.

THEAETETUS, *a young Athenian.*

THEODORUS *of Cyrene, a geometrician, teacher of* THEAETETUS.

The scene opens in front of EUCLID'S *house in Megara, where* EUCLID *and* TERPSION *meet. The reading of the dialogue takes place within the house.*

THEAETETUS.

Euclid. Just arrived, Terpsion, or are you long in from the country?

Terpsion. Tolerably long. And you — I was looking for you in the Agora,[1] and wondering that I did not find you there.

Euc. But I was not in the city.

Terp. Where then?

Euc. On my way down to the harbour, I met Theaetetus, who was being carried to Athens from the camp before Corinth.[2]

Terp. Alive or dead?

Euc. Alive, but barely so; for not only does it go hard with him from his wounds, but, what is worse, the disease which has broken out in the army is upon him.

Terp. Surely not the dysentery!

Euc. Yes.

Terp. What a man is this who you say is in danger!

Euc. A true and gallant one indeed, Terpsion! Only just now I heard great praises of his behaviour in the battle.

Terp. That is not strange; on the contrary, it would have been more surprising if you had not heard them. But how comes it that he did not stop here at Megara?

Euc. He was bent upon getting home. I entreated him, you may be sure, and advised him to stay, but he would not. And I may tell you that, on my way back from escorting him, I remembered the words of Socrates, and marvelled at the prophetic insight shown by him in this as in other matters. It was, I think, shortly before his own death that he met Theaetetus, — then a mere stripling, — and was greatly impressed by his natural ability, after they had been together and conversed awhile. And when I came to Athens, he repeated to me the conversation he had had with him, — and well worth hearing it was, — and declared that Theaetetus would undoubtedly make a name for himself, if he lived to reach man's estate.

Terp. And he spoke the truth, it seems. But what was the conversation? Could you manage to repeat it?

Euc. No, by Zeus; at least not thus from memory. But as soon as I got home I made notes, and afterward as, at my leisure, I recalled more I would write it out. Then, whenever I went to Athens, I used to ask Socrates what I had not been able to recollect, and to set it right upon my return; so that I have nearly the whole conversation written out.

Terp. True. I have heard you mention this before; in fact, I have always intended asking you to show it me, but have put off doing so till this moment. But is there any reason why we should not go over it now? For my part I am really in need of rest, having walked in from the country.

Euc. Why, I myself escorted Theaetetus as far as Erineum;[3] so that I should not be sorry to rest, either. Suppose we go in; and as we take our ease, the boy shall read aloud to us.

Terp. A good suggestion.[4]

Euc. Here you have the scroll, Terpsion. I must tell you that I wrote down the conversation, not as if it were being related to me by Socrates, which was actually the case, but as if he were speaking to those with whom he said he had talked, — Theodorus the geometrician,[5] and our Theaetetus. And, to avoid the troublesome connecting links between the parts of the dialogue, — as when for instance Socrates says of himself, "I then said," or "I remarked," or again of the person answering, that "he agreed," or "here he refused assent," — I have set everything down as if he were actually talking with them, and have struck out all the rest.

Terp. That is not at all out of the way, Euclid.

Euc. Well, boy, take the scroll and read.

The servant of Euclid reads.

Socrates. If I had the affairs of Cyrene more at heart, Theodorus, I should question you in regard to men and matters there, — whether any of the youths are turning their attention to geometry or to any other study. But as it is, I care less for those youths than for our own, and am far more concerned to know which of our young men are likely to make a name for themselves; so that I am on the lookout myself, as far as may be, and am always questioning others when I observe that young men like their society. Now not a few of them are followers of yours, and rightly too, such is your reputation for knowledge on all subjects, especially geometry. So if you have come across any one worth the mention, I should be glad to know of it.

Theodorus. Yes, Socrates, I have come across a certain youth, one of your fellow-citizens, who does indeed deserve being brought to your notice. Really, if he were handsome I should be afraid to speak as strongly as I feel, lest it might be supposed I were in love with him. But in point of fact, — now don't be angry with me! — he is not handsome, but is very like you in the flatness of his nose and the setting of his eyes, although this is less marked in him than in you;[6] and so I may speak without fear. You must know, then, that of all the people I have ever met, — and I have associated with many, — I never found any one so marvellously endowed by nature. The ease with which he acquires what is difficult to others, his peculiar gentleness, and, to crown all, his surpassing courage, — such a combination I should not have supposed possible, nor do I know of any similar one.[7] For they who, like him, are keen and quick-witted and have a strong memory are also for the most part quickly moved to anger, and are unresistingly swept along as ships without ballast, being more like madmen than men of courage; while they who have more poise bring to their studies a sluggish spirit, and are weighted with forgetfulness. Whereas so calmly and steadily and effectually does he set about his studies and investigations, and so quietly withal, — like the noiseless flow of a stream of oil, — that it is marvellous how one of his age can accomplish all this as he does.

Soc. You give us good news; and which of our citizens is his father?

Theod. I have heard the name, but I do not remember it. However, the youth himself is one of those just entering over there, — the one in the middle. He and some of his companions were just anointing themselves in the outer race-course,[8] but they seem now to have finished and to be coming this way. See if you know him.

Soc. Yes, I know him. He is the son of Euphronius of Sunium, who was just such a man, my friend, as you describe this youth to be, and universally esteemed, and who also, now I think of it, left a large property. But the young fellow's name I do not know.

Theod. Theaetetus is his name, Socrates.

The property, I believe, certain guardians of his have made away with; but for all that, Socrates, he is remarkable for his liberality, with money as well as in other matters.

Soc. As you describe him he is a noble fellow. Pray bid him come here and sit down by me.

Theod. That I will. Theaetetus, come here and sit by Socrates.⁹

Soc. Yes, Theaetetus, pray do, that I may gaze upon myself and see what manner of face I have; for Theodorus tells me that mine is like yours.

[Socrates and Theaetetus soon come to the conclusion that since Theodorus is no painter, his opinion as to likeness or unlikeness of face does not deserve much attention.]

145 B. *Soc.* But how if it were the mind of one of us two that he was praising for virtue and wisdom? Would it not be right for the one eagerly to study him who is praised, and for the other with equal eagerness to exhibit himself?

Theaet. By all means, Socrates.

Soc. This then, dear Theaetetus, is the moment for you to exhibit, and for me to observe you; for you must know that although Theodorus has praised many a man to me, both stranger and citizen, he has never yet praised any one as he did you just now.

Theaet. It is pleasant to hear that, Socrates; but have a care! He may have been joking.

Soc. That is not in character with Theodorus. So pray do not draw back from your agreement, under the pretext that he was in joke, or he himself will be forced to bear me witness, and his word no one will ever call in question. No, you had better stand boldly by the agreement.

Theaet. Well, I suppose I must, if you wish it.

[Socrates now bespeaks the aid of Theaetetus and the rest of the company in the solution of what he calls a "little matter of perplexity," and introduces it as follows:]

Soc. Here, then, is the question that I am puzzled about and cannot by myself fully grasp: *What is knowledge?* Is it a thing possible to define? What say you? Which of us will speak first? Whichever of us misses, and whenever he misses, shall, as the children say when they play at ball, sit down a donkey. But he who comes off victorious, without once missing, shall be king over us, and shall give out whatever question he pleases. — Why are you silent? I trust, Theodorus, that my fondness for argument has not led me to commit any rudeness, in my anxiety that we should all take part in the conversation and become friendly and familiar together.

Theod. No indeed, Socrates, such a wish is

far from rude; but pray bid one of the younger ones answer you. For I have no experience in debate of this kind, and, moreover, am not of an age to accustom myself to it; whereas it would suit them and they would make much better progress, for youth is capable of progress in everything. And so, having begun with Theaetetus, do not let him off, but go on questioning him.

Soc. Well, Theaetetus, you hear what Theodorus says, whom I imagine you would be loath to disobey; nor indeed is it right for one who is so much younger to disobey the commands of a man experienced in matters of this kind. Speak out then frankly and fearlessly. What do you understand by knowledge?

Theaet. Well, Socrates, since you both bid me answer, I suppose I must. And of course if I make a false step you will set me right.

Soc. Certainly we shall, — that is, if we can.

[146 C.–148 B. Theaetetus begins by enumerating the different arts and sciences, but is cut short by the reminder of Socrates that a general notion of knowledge itself, not the various applications thereof, is the object of their search. He then bethinks him of a certain geometrical generalization worked out recently by himself and his friend, the younger Socrates. This he proceeds to give, much to the admiration of his hearer, who exclaims:]

Soc. Capital, my boys! No one could have done better! Small danger now that Theodorus will be accused of bearing false witness!

Theaet. But I assure you, Socrates, that I could never answer your question about knowledge, as I did that about linear measurement and square root, and yet it is, I imagine, something of this kind that you are looking for. And thus again it looks as if Theodorus were a deceiver.

Soc. How so? Suppose he had praised your running, and declared that he had never met a youth who was such a swift runner; and suppose you were afterward worsted in a race by one who, besides being swift, was in the prime of life,— would his praise, think you, be any the less true?

Theaet. No, I do not think it would.

Soc. And do you think that knowledge is, as I said just now, a slight thing to be discovered, and not one of the loftiest of all things in the world?

Theaet. Nay, by Zeus, I think it is; one of the very loftiest.

Soc. Take heart, then, about yourself, and believe that Theodorus is right, and strive in every way to apprehend the true nature of knowledge, and of all other things.

Theaet. If it is only a question of striving, Socrates, it shall be brought to light.

Soc. Come, then: you gave a capital example just now. Taking pattern by the answer you gave about square roots, endeavour, as you brought all these, many as they are, under one head, to include in the same way the many forms of knowledge under one name.

Theaet. But you must know, Socrates, that many a time, when I have heard questions repeated of your asking, I have tried to do this very thing. I cannot convince myself, however, that I have any satisfactory statement to make, nor have I heard anybody else make such a one as you call for; and yet I cannot get rid of my concern about it.

Soc. That is because you are in travail, dear Theaetetus, and your mind is big with thought.

Theaet. I do not know how that is, Socrates. I only tell you how I feel.

Soc. Can it be, my simple friend, that you have never heard me spoken of as the son of a midwife, strong and sturdy, Phaenarete by name?

Theaet. Why, yes, this I have heard.

Soc. And that I practise the same art,— have you heard this too?

Theaet. No, never.

Soc. Know then that I do. But do not, I beg of you, betray me to others, for they, my friend, are not aware that I possess the art; and not knowing it, they do not say this of me, but what they do say is that I am the strangest of mortals, and that I bring men to their wits' end.[10] This you have heard, have you not?

Theaet. Yes, I have.

[149 B.–150 C. In the well-known passage which follows, Socrates brings out various points of resemblance between his mother's profession and his own office of helping men to evolve their own thoughts.]

Soc. Now I am certainly not especially wise myself, nor has any discovery been born to me, as the offspring of my own mind. But it is nevertheless true of those who come to me, that although at the outset some of them show themselves ignorant, and even surprisingly so, yet as our intercourse goes on, they all — those at least to whom the god is favourable — make the most amazing progress; and this not only in their own opinion but in that of others as well. And it is as clear as day that what they have learned was never of my teaching, but that they have discovered of themselves the many noble truths which they attain, although for the bringing of them forth the god and I myself are responsible. . . .

151 D. Go back, then, Theaetetus, to the beginning, and try to define what knowledge is. And never once admit that you are not able. For if God be favourable, and you show a manful spirit, you will be able.

Theaet. Indeed, Socrates, after such an exhortation from you, it would be shameful if one did not use every effort to speak out that which is within him. Well, it seems to me that he who knows anything perceives the thing that he knows; and therefore knowledge, so far as I can at present see, is nothing else than perception.[11]

Soc. Well and nobly said, my boy! That is the right way to speak out your thoughts.

[151 D.–155 C. Further examination shows that in identifying knowledge with perception, or the transitory and changing impression produced by objects, Theaetetus is in accord with Protagoras, Heraclitus, Empedocles,[12] and indeed all the other philosophers, save Parmenides. The famous maxim of Protagoras, " Man is the measure of all things; as they seem to him, so they are," is but one with the theory of Heraclitus, that " nothing in reality exists, but is ever becoming." And even Homer expresses the same idea when he sings of " Ocean, creator of gods and Tethys the mother," meaning thereby that all things are engendered by flux and motion. But the theory, although apparently borne out by many phenomena in physical and mental life, does yet abound in extraordinary contradictions: if, for example, taking six dice, we compare them with four others, their number is increased; if with twelve, it is diminished. " Suppose then," Socrates continues, " that Protagoras or any one else were to ask you, ' Is there anything, Theaetetus, that grows larger or smaller except by growth?' what would you answer?"

154 C. "If my answer, Socrates, is to agree with the present form of the question, I should say

'no;' if I am to take care not to contradict my former answer, 'yes.'"

"Well spoken, by Hera, my friend, and even divinely. But yet if you do reply 'yes,' you will find yourself in the same case with Euripides: 'The tongue will be convinced, but not the mind.'" [13]

"I assume, Theaetetus," Socrates adds, after amplifying this and similar contradictions, "that you follow me, for you seem to me not unfamiliar with questions of this kind."]

Theaet. Yes, and by the gods, Socrates, I do wonder exceedingly what it all means. Sometimes, indeed, when I contemplate these things, I turn positively giddy.

Soc. It is evident, my friend, that Theodorus made no bad guess as to your character. For this very thing — wonder — is an affection peculiar to the philosophic mind. In truth, philosophy has no beginning save this; and he who said that Iris was the offspring of wonder proved himself, methinks, no bad hand at tracing pedigree.[14] But do you now understand why these things are the result of what we call the doctrine of Protagoras, or do you not as yet?

Theaet. Not yet, I think.

Soc. Well, will you be grateful to me if I aid you in drawing out the truth hidden away in the mind of a man, or rather men, of renown?

Theaet. How could I but be grateful, and in large measure too?

Soc. But first look about carefully, lest we be overheard by one of the uninitiated, — they, I mean, who do not admit the existence of anything which they cannot hold fast in their two hands, and who do not believe that action and generation and all that is unseen can be classed as really existent.[15]

Theaet. The men of whom you speak, Socrates, are hard and stubborn indeed.

156

[156 A.–160 E. Socrates proceeds to examine the hypothesis upon which the doctrine of the school of Protagoras is founded.

On being asked whether he does not "relish the taste of these theories," Theaetetus replies:

157 C. "For my part, Socrates, I do not know, for I cannot make out whether you believe it all yourself, or are only drawing me out." And he adds: "When I hear you going on thus, it does, I confess, seem to me that there is marvellous reason in it, and that all you have set forth must be accepted."

"Let us then," Socrates urges, "not abandon what remains unfinished of the subject, such as its aspect in relation to dreams and diseases, and especially madness and its delusions of sight, hearing, and other senses, . . . in all which cases appearances are the reverse of what they seem.".

Still speaking in the name of those who hold appearances to be the truth, Socrates declares that knowledge is not absolute, but relative, nothing, in fact, having reality save in its relation to some percipient. Thus the same food which to the well man is sweet, is bitter to the sick, nor is the latter to be deemed the more ignorant of the two, because of the difference in his perception. And hereby is justified the saying of Protagoras, "I am judge of all things."

"Admirable indeed," so Socrates reviews the situation, "is your assertion that knowledge is nothing but perception; and it comes to the same thing whether, with Homer and Heraclitus and all that set, you say that all things are flux and motion; or with Protagoras, wisest of all men, that man is the measure of all things; or with Theaetetus, that perception is knowledge."]

Soc. Is it not so, Theaetetus? May we not say that this is, as it were, your new-born child? ... Must he, think you, be reared at all hazards and on no account put away? Or can you bear to see him proved spurious, and not be exceeding wroth if any one takes from you your first-born?

Theod. Theaetetus will bear it, Socrates, for he is not in the least irritable. But by the gods tell me, is this in its turn untrue?

Soc. You are certainly a lover of argument, Theodorus, and a simple fellow to boot, if you think that I am in some sort a bagful of arguments and can easily draw one out to prove that these things are not true after all. But you do not see the real state of the case, — that not a single one of the arguments comes from me, but invariably from him who is talking with me, and that I myself only understand this one simple thing, — how I may apprehend and accept in a spirit of fairness the argument of some other man who is wise. And so I shall try to get one now out of our philosopher here, and not speak at all myself.

Theod. That is the better way, Socrates; pray do as you say.

Soc. Well, Theodorus, do you know what surprises me in your friend Protagoras?

[161 C.-162 A. The matter for surprise is this: If it be true that all men are equally capable of forming a right judgment, how can any one man, even Protagoras himself, be held as pre-eminent and therefore fit for the guidance of others? Nay, why should not any animal who is gifted with perception be also pronounced a "measure of all things"? This attack upon his old master's fundamental principle is used by Theodorus as an excuse for not taking part in the discussion.]

Theod. The man was a friend of mine, Socrates, as you have just said. I therefore should neither be willing on the one hand to have Protagoras refuted by my admissions, nor on the other to oppose you against my own conviction. Pray, then, try Theaetetus again. Surely he seemed to be answering very suitably just now.

Soc. Suppose, Theodorus, you were to go into the palaestras at Lacedemon, should you think it fair, when the other people were naked, — some of them, by the way, poor specimens enough, — not to strip yourself also, and let your figure be compared with theirs?

Theod. Why, don't you suppose that I should, if I could persuade them to let me? And just so I shall now, I think, persuade you to let me look on, and, instead of dragging me into the gymnasium now that I have grown stiff, to try yourself against some younger and more supple opponent in my place.

Soc. Why, of course, Theodorus, friend to you cannot be foe to me, as the proverb has it. So let us, by all means, go back to our wise Theaetetus. First then, referring to the matter just under discussion, tell me, Theaetetus, are you not amazed if you are to be suddenly proved inferior in wisdom to none, whether men or even gods? Or do you suppose that the measure of Protagoras applies less to gods than to men?

Theaet. Not I, by Zeus! To answer your question, I am indeed greatly amazed. When we were considering the doctrine that what "seems" to each man "is" really so to him, I thought it admirable. But now of a sudden, all is reversed.

Soc. That is because you are young, dear boy,

and therefore quick to hear and to be convinced by popular talk.

[162 D.–168 E. Theaetetus is now urged not to rest satisfied until his own and the Protagorean theory has been examined under another aspect. If perception be really identical with knowledge, what shall we say of things that we perceive, but do not know, such as letters in a foreign language which, though seen, are not understood by us?

163 C. "We shall say," replies Theaetetus, "that what we actually see and hear of them we do understand, — that is, we see and understand their form and colour, and we hear and recognize their rising and falling inflections, — but what the grammarians and interpreters teach about them, we neither perceive nor know, whether by sight or hearing."

"That is excellent, Theaetetus!" cries Socrates; "I will not stop to argue the point with you, because I want to let you grow. But look! here comes something else, which we must consider how we may fight against."

The "something else" is the knowledge which comes from memory. If by means of this we can continue to know what we no longer see, it follows that perception can be no essential part of knowledge; and thus the fable of Protagoras is seen to be forever destroyed.

164 E. "And yet, my friend," Socrates adds, "I

doubt not that, were the father of the aforesaid fable still alive, he would have had much to say in its defence. But now, since it is an orphan, we are heaping abuse upon it. Nor do even the guardians whom Protagoras left in charge, care to give their help, as, for instance, Theodorus here. And so, for the sake of fair play, it seems that we ourselves must come to the rescue."

"It is not I, Socrates, who am guardian," Theodorus pleads in excuse, "but rather Callias, the son of Hipponicus. For I was earlier than he turned aside from abstract questions to the study of geometry. If you, however, will come to the rescue, I shall be very grateful."

Socrates accordingly, impersonating the old philosopher, declares, in his name, that truth is an ever-varying quality. Thus an evil mind sees no less truly than does a good one, for a man's own experience is to him the only reality, nor can he possibly grasp anything outside of it. A good man, nevertheless, has the power so to change the condition of another's mind, that opinions like his own may be generated there in place of evil ones. In like manner wise and good rhetoricians have power in the state to make the good not only discerned, but chosen in preference to the evil. At the close of his defence, Protagoras expresses disapproval of the unfair and frivolous spirit shown by his adversary, whose method has been that of disputation rather than of argument.]

168 C. *Soc.* Thus, Theodorus, have I to the best of my ability contributed to the defence of your friend, — slight help from slight source. Had he been alive himself, he would have defended his own in far more stately fashion.

Theod. You are jesting, Socrates, for you have defended him right valiantly.

Soc. That is kind of you, my friend. But tell me, — did you, I wonder, when Protagoras was speaking just now, notice how he upbraided us, because by addressing our discourse to a boy, we were making the boy's timidity a weapon against his own arguments; and how he denounced this as a sorry kind of jest; and how, holding up to our admiration his "measure of all things," he bade us address ourselves to his doctrine in sober earnest?

Theod. How could I help noticing it, Socrates?

Soc. Well, do you advise us to obey him?

Theod. I do, emphatically.

Soc. But don't you see that all here present, with the exception of yourself, are children? If then we are to obey the man, you and I must apply ourselves seriously to his doctrine, and address our questions and answers to one another, so that he may at least not have occasion to reproach us with again turning our study of his doctrine into a frolic with boys.

Theod. What! would not Theaetetus follow the investigation of a doctrine better than many a man with a long beard?

Soc. But not better, Theodorus, than yourself. Pray do not imagine that it is my duty to stand up for your departed friend in every way, and yours in no way whatever. So come, my good fellow, follow this matter just a little further, that we may see whether you are to be the measure of diagrams, or whether all other men are, equally with you, sufficient unto themselves in astronomy and all other branches wherein you are reputed to excel.

Theod. It is not easy, Socrates, for one seated by your side to get off from rendering an account of himself, and I was talking nonsense just now when I said you would excuse me from stripping myself, and would not rather, like the Lacedaemonians, force me into doing it; although you, to be sure, seem rather to take after Sciron. For the Lacedaemonians command one either to strip or to go away, while you, methinks, do the business rather after the fashion of Antaeus: if a man is once within your reach, you will not let him go till you have compelled him both to strip and to try himself against you in argument.[16]

Soc. You have described my malady perfectly, Theodorus, only I am a far more doughty opponent than they. For many a Heracles and a Theseus mighty in the art of controversy has ere now fallen upon me and given me a sound drubbing; but none the more for that do I desist, so strongly am I imbued with a love for this kind of exercise. Pray, then, do not refuse to close in with me, for your own good no less than for mine.

Theod. I will make no further opposition. Lead whithersoever you will; in any case I shall have to bear, by cross-examination, whatever fate you spin for me. But I warn you that I shall not be able to go beyond the limit proposed by you.

Soc. That far is quite sufficient; and pray give your utmost heed that we do not unconsciously fall into any childish fashion of talking, and again bring that reproach upon ourselves.

Theod. I will certainly try, so far as I can.

[169 D.–172 C. The investigation now assuming a more serious character, the conclusion is finally reached that to confess every man's opinions the "measure of all things" is to acknowledge your own to be in error, inasmuch as certain other opinions will surely be at variance with them; neither, it is added, can any man be the measure of a thing which he has not learned. And thus the famous truth of Protagoras is true neither to the discoverer of it nor to any one else.

171 C. "Ah, but, Socrates," cries Theodorus, "we are running my friend very hard."

"But I really do not see, my dear fellow," Socrates rejoins, "that we are outrunning what is right. Though it is likely, to be sure, that being older he is also wiser than ourselves; and if he could at this moment thrust his head up from yonder where he is, he would soon, I doubt not, convict me of talking great nonsense, and you of accepting the same, and then down he would sink and be off again in a trice.[17] But all the same we must, it seems to me, use our own faculties, such as they are, and always say what we think."

It soon becomes apparent, however applicable may be the doctrine of Protagoras in matters of right and wrong, that in questions of expediency, both present and future, whether in matters of State or in private affairs, all men are not equally capable of right judgment.]

Soc. But here from one question, Theodorus, we are being forced into another, — from a lesser into a greater one.

Theod. Well, Socrates, we have plenty of time, have we not?

Soc. Apparently so. In truth, my good fellow, I have often before reflected, just as I am doing now, how natural it is that they who have spent much time in the study of philosophy should cut a ridiculous figure when they come to speak in court.[18]

Theod. Exactly what do you mean?

Soc. I mean that, in point of breeding, those who from earliest youth have knocked about in law courts and places of that kind are, compared with those trained in philosophy and other such pursuits, like slaves in comparison with free men.

Theod. In what way?

Soc. In that the leisure you spoke of is always at the command of the philosophers. They have their argument out in peace and at leisure; and just as we now for the third time are changing from one subject to another, so do they also, if, like us, they prefer to discuss a subject which comes later in order rather than the matter in hand. And they care not whether they speak briefly or at length, if only they get at the truth. Whereas the others always talk in a hurry,—for the running of the water drives them on,—and they have not time to speak on what they have at heart; while there the opponent stands armed with the constraining power of a written brief outside of which they dare not speak,—the so-called affidavits.[19] And their talk is always about some fellow-slave, and is addressed to the master who sits holding in his hand the penalty to be awarded; and the trial is never about some indifferent matter, but always about the speaker himself,—and ofttimes the race is for life. From all these causes they become sharp and shrewd, and apt at flattering the master by word and courting his favour by deed, and their souls are stunted and not upright. For slavery from childhood takes away all growth and self-respect and freedom, and makes crooked deeds a necessity, and surrounds with great fears and dangers souls which, being as yet tender, are unable to pass through them save at the expense of justice and truth. And, having straightway recourse to falsehood and retaliation, they become so cramped and warped that by the time they have passed from youth to man's estate their minds have no longer any soundness in them, though in their own opinion they have become both wise and capable. Such, Theodorus, are these men. And now what do you wish? Shall we describe those of our chorus,[20] or shall we dismiss this subject and go back to our discussion, lest we take undue advantage of that liberty and free exchange of intercourse which we were talking about just now?

Theod. On no account, Socrates; pray let us have the whole. For you were quite right in declaring that we who belong to such a chorus as this are not the slaves of our own words; but our arguments are, so to speak, servants of ours, each waiting to be perfected when it shall seem to us good. For neither judge nor spectator stands over us, as with the poets, to censure or control.

Soc. Very well, since it so pleases you, we will speak of the leaders; for what need to speak of those who only dabble superficially in philosophy? In the first place, then, from youth up they have never so much as known their way to the Agora, nor yet to the courts of justice or the council hall or any other public place of assembly. Laws and ordinances, whether they be written or spoken, they neither see nor hear.

Struggles of political leagues for leadership, assemblies, banquets, revelries with flute-girls, — it does not occur to them, even in their dreams, to take part in these. Whether matters have gone well or ill in the State, whether misfortune has come to any one from ancestors on the male or the female line,[21] he is more ignorant of than of how many gallons are said to be contained in the sea. Nor is he even conscious that he does not know these things, as it is not for the sake of gaining repute that he holds aloof; but the truth is that his body alone is placed in the city and there abides, while his soul, regarding all this as petty and of no account, and "borne," in the words of Pindar, "hither and thither,"[22] takes measure of things on the earth, and under the earth, and observes the stars in the heavens, and 174 searches out the nature of every created being, each in its entirety, stooping to none of those which lie close at hand.

Theod. How do you mean, Socrates?

Soc. I mean, Theodorus, after the fashion of Thales, who gazing up at the stars tumbled into a well;[23] on which occasion a clever and quick-witted Thracian handmaid is reputed to have scoffingly said that in his eagerness to know what was going on in heaven he did not notice what lay in front of him, beneath his very feet. And the same raillery serves for all who pursue philosophy. A man of this sort is in truth ignorant of both friend and neighbour, — not only of what he is doing, but almost whether he is a human being or some other creature. But when it comes to what man really is, and what it befits such a nature as his to do or to suffer, in distinction from all others, — this he is ever investigating and sparing no pains to discover. You understand me, Theodorus, I suppose, — or do you not?

Theod. Yes, indeed; and what you say is true.

Soc. Consequently, my friend, when a man of this kind comes into relation with others, — whether, as I said before, in private or on a public occasion, — when, in a court of justice or elsewhere, he is forced to talk of things which lie beneath his feet and before his very eyes, he makes himself a laughing-stock not to Thracian handmaids only, but to the crowd in general; and by reason of his inexperience he tumbles into wells and every other kind of perplexity; and his excessive awkwardness makes him appear like a fool. For when insulted, he can retort no insulting personalities, because, never having paid attention to such matters, he knows no harm of any one; and so, in this quandary, he cuts a ridiculous figure. And when, on hearing others praised and lauded, he is seen to be laughing, not affectedly but in good earnest, he is set down as a simpleton.

But the fact is, when a king or a tyrant is commended it seems to him like congratulating some herdsman, — perhaps a swineherd, or a shepherd, or some cowherd because he has many creatures to milk; only he thinks that the animal which the tyrant has to tend and milk is far more treacherous and choleric than is the herdsman's charge, and that a man of this kind is, from want of leisure, no less rough and uneducated than the herdsman, — being girt about by a wall, his mountain fold.

Does he hear the owner of ten thousand or more acres spoken of as possessing a vast property, he regards it as a mere nothing, so accustomed is he to embrace within his view the whole earth. Do they extol pedigree, — saying how such a one is noble because he can boast of wealthy ancestors for seven generations back,— it seems to him that the commendation can proceed only from persons of dull and contracted vision, who by reason of ignorance are not able to embrace the whole within their ken, nor to consider that every one of us has had thousands untold of ancestors and progenitors, among whom there are in every case rich men and beggars, kings and slaves, Greeks and barbarians, many times ten thousand for every one. That men should pride themselves upon a list of twenty-five ancestors, and go back to Heracles, the son of Amphitryon, is to him a sign of extreme pettiness; and inasmuch as the twenty-fifth ancestor back of Amphitryon was just what fortune made him, and also the fiftieth before him again, he laughs to think that they have not the wit to reckon this up, and thus put an end to the vain glory of a foolish mind.[24]

In all these cases a man of this kind is laughed at by the crowd, because while as to some things he appears haughty, as to others he does not know what lies beneath his feet, and is helpless when it comes to details.

Theod. You describe everything just as it is, Socrates.

Soc. But when he himself, my friend, draws another up to his own height, — one who is willing to rise with him beyond the question of " In what way do I injure you or you me?" to the examination of righteousness and injustice in themselves, — what each of these is, and wherein they differ from each other and from all things else, — or from the question, " Is a monarch happy because he has great wealth?" to the consideration of monarchy itself and the sum of human happiness and misery, — what each of these consists in, and in what manner the nature of man is fitted to acquire the one and avoid the other, — when that little, dried up pettifogger's soul has to give an answer to all these questions, then indeed does he give the philosopher his revenge. Dizzied by the unwonted experience of hanging from such heights and gazing downward through the air, distressed, confused, and stammering, he is a laughing-stock, not to Thracian handmaids nor to any of the ignorant, — they do not even perceive it, — but to all who have been brought up not as slaves, but in the opposite fashion.[25]

Such, Theodorus, is the character of these two, — the one, called by you philosopher, who, brought up in freedom and leisure, may well be excused if he appear helpless and incompetent when some slavish task devolves upon him, as when for example he does not know how to pack up his bedding or to flavour a sauce or a flattering phrase; the other, who is able to perform deftly and quickly all such tasks, but does not know how to throw his cloak over his shoulder like a free man,[26] still less how to make choice of fitting speech wherewith to celebrate worthily the true life lived of gods and of men blessed of heaven.

Theod. Ah, Socrates, if your words could only persuade others as they do me, there would be more peace and less evil among men!

Soc. But it is not possible, Theodorus, to destroy evil, for the opposite of good must needs always exist; nor is its abiding-place to be imagined among the gods, for it hovers of necessity about mortal nature here below. Therefore it behooves us to make good our escape hence to yonder place as fast as may be. And the way of escape is this, — to grow as like unto God as possible; and to grow like him is to become just and holy, and wise withal.[27] But in sooth, my friend, it is far from easy to persuade people that not for the reason which most men give for cultivating virtue and not vice, — namely, to make a good instead of a bad appearance, — not for this reason, I say, is the one to be shunned and the other pursued. For this, it seems to me, is nothing but an oft repeated old wives' tale.

But the truth we will proclaim in this wise: God is never in any wise unjust, for he is perfectly just, and there is nothing more like him than the man among us who has made himself the most just. Upon this depends the real ability of a man, or else his nothingness and unmanliness. The knowledge of this truth is wisdom and true virtue, the ignorance of it sheer stupidity and vice; and all else that looks like cleverness and wisdom is in matters of politics mere coarseness, in the arts vulgarity.

It is far better, then, never to admit that he who is unrighteous and profane in talk and behaviour is clever by reason of his villany. Such men glory in this reproach, and flatter themselves that they are regarded not as mere fools and cumberers of the ground,[28] but as patterns for all men who wish to live with safety in a state. But they must be told the truth, — they are all the more what they believe they are not, for the very reason that they hold this belief. For they know not the reward of unrighteousness, a thing which least of all others they ought to be ignorant of, and which is not, as they imagine, stripes and death, — evils frequently not incurred by those who have done wrong, — but something impossible to escape from.

Theod. What do you mean?

Soc. Two living types, my friend, are set before them, — the one divine and of perfect blessedness, the other with naught of the divine and of utter misery. But this they do not perceive, and their excessive folly and stupidity makes them unconscious that on account of their evil deeds they are growing like the one and unlike the other. And the penalty they pay is that the life led by them is in the likeness of that which they resemble. If we tell them that unless they get rid of their boasted cleverness, they will not, even when dead, be received into that place which is free from evil, but must ever continue here upon earth in that way of life which is like unto themselves, — evil consorting with evil,[29] — they will listen to us, but only as clever knaves might listen to a set of fools.

Theod. Indeed they will, Socrates.

Soc. I am quite aware of it, my friend. There is, however, this about them, that if they are confronted with one person alone, and made to give their reasons in regard to what they censure, — that is, if they are willing to stand their ground and not run away like cowards, — they end, my good sir, by becoming strangely dissatisfied with their own reasons; and that famous rhetoric of theirs shrivels away, as it were, so that they seem no better than children.

But all these are mere digressions, and we had best restrain ourselves, or we shall have yet more of them flowing in to choke up our main argument. If you approve, therefore, we will return to our former subject.

Theod. For my own part, Socrates, I do not find it at all unpleasant to listen to such digressions as these, for they are easier for one of my age to understand. But still, if you wish it, we will go back again.

[177 C.-179 E. The discussion is now resumed at the point where it was interrupted by the digression. That some men are wiser than others, and that the wiser man alone can be a fit " measure," is at last fully conceded by Theodorus.

It still remains to be considered whether in the matter of momentary impressions also each man's judgment is infallible. Such a supposition would seem to be supported by the theory of a universal flux or continual change and motion, and the Heracliteans are accordingly summoned, though not without a protest from Theodorus, who declares that they are " no more possible to deal with than madmen."]

Theod. For in accordance with their own compositions, they are forever in motion; and as for carrying on an argument, and quietly questioning and answering by turn,—this to them is nothing short of impossible. . . . On the contrary, if one of them is asked a question, he pulls forth, as from a quiver, some enigmatical saying and shoots it out. And if you try to get at the meaning of what he has said, you will be struck down by some other new-fangled saying, but with none of these men will you ever arrive at any conclusion; nor, for that matter, will they do so with one another, for they are exceedingly wary of admitting anything as fixed, — whether in argument or in their own souls, — on the supposition, I believe, that to be fixed is to be stationary; against which principle they wage fierce war and drive it out wherever they can.

Soc. Apparently, Theodorus, you have seen these men in a state of warfare, and have never had anything to do with them in time of peace, as they are not intimates of yours. But I imagine that, when quietly by themselves, they do impart ideas of another kind to their disciples, whom they desire to make like themselves.

Theod. Disciples, indeed, my good sir! None of that sort are ever disciples one of the other. No, indeed, they grow up of their own accord, each getting inspiration wherever he may chance upon it, and each one thinking that the other knows nothing. No, from these, as I was about to say, you will never get any explanation, either with their consent or without it.[30] We must perforce take the doctrine up ourselves, and consider it as we would a problem.

[180 C.–183 B. Upon the theory of universal motion, all things are not only forever changing place, but are also continually undergoing change of condition. To admit this doctrine, therefore, is to deny the possibility of impressions; since before there is time to receive an impression, the object itself will have changed. After some further parley the doctrine of Protagoras and of the Heracliteans is finally dismissed as untenable.]

Soc. So, then, Theodorus, we have got rid of your friend, and do not as yet agree with him that every one is the measure of all things, except indeed he be some wise man; nor will we agree either that knowledge is perception, at least not on the doctrine of universal motion. But perhaps Theaetetus here has something more to propose.

Theod. You have spoken capitally, Socrates; so much so that I must be now released from the obligation of answering you, as it was agreed I should be, whenever our talk about the doctrine of Protagoras was at an end.

Theaet. But not, Theodorus, before you and Socrates, as you proposed awhile ago, have reviewed the doctrine of those who maintain that everything is at rest.

Theod. So young, Theaetetus, and yet teaching your elders to act unjustly and break their faith! Nay, rather get ready to answer Socrates yourself during the rest of the discussion.

Theaet. Of course, if he desires it. But I would much rather have listened, as I said.

Theod. It is challenging horsemen upon an open plain, to challenge Socrates to argument. Only question him and you will hear.

Soc. On the contrary, Theodorus, I do not think I shall obey the request of Theaetetus.

Theod. But why will you not obey it?

Soc. Such is my reverence for Melissus and the others, who hold that the universe is one and moveless, that I am ashamed to examine these doctrines in an unworthy manner. But I feel this less with them than with Parmenides, the One.[31] For, to my thinking, Parmenides is, in the words of Homer, "venerable at once and awesome." I met the man when he was very aged and I a very young lad, and to me the depth of his mind seemed altogether magnificent. I fear therefore that we may not understand even his words, and may be left still farther behind as to his meaning; and more than all am I fearful that other questions, if once allowed, will force themselves in, and prevent us from considering that which was the starting-point of our discussion, — the nature of knowledge. . . .

Let us try, then, by the help of our art, to deliver Theaetetus of his conceptions in regard to knowledge.

Theod. By all means do so, if you think it best.

[184 B.-191 E. Returning to the original definition, Socrates questions the accuracy of the common statement, — that sight and sound are discerned *with* the eyes and ears. "A free use of words and phrases," he declares, "is for the most part a sign of breeding; a too punctilious accuracy is, on the other hand, underbred. Sometimes however, as on the present occasion, where a statement is not correct it must needs be called in question. Consider, then, which is more correct, — that we see *with* the eyes or *by means* of the eyes, and hear *with* the ears or *by means* of the ears?"

"It seems to me, Socrates," is the reply, "that we perceive *by means* of our organs rather than *with* them."

"Yes," Socrates rejoins; "for it were indeed strange if, as though we were so many Trojan horses, there were placed within us a quantity of senses, but no one general principle, whether it be called soul or anything else, to which they all tend and with which, albeit by means of these senses as instruments, we perceive all objects that can be perceived."[32]

The conclusion is finally reached that, although tangible objects are noted by the help of the senses, abstract ideas, — such as being and non-being, likeness and unlikeness, identity and difference, — are perceived by no bodily organ, but by the soul alone; whereupon with a burst of enthusiasm Socrates exclaims:

185 E. "You are beautiful, Theaetetus, and not ugly, as Theodorus says; for he who speaks beautiful words is himself both beautiful and good. And besides being beautiful, you are doing me a kindness by sparing me a long discussion; that is, if you believe that the soul perceives some things by her own power alone, and others by the help of bodily organs.[33] For this was my own belief and what I was wishing might be yours also.

It is now demonstrated that our knowledge of the essential part of things — what we call the realities — is derived, not from the senses, but from the reflections made by the soul upon the report of the senses; and that perception which is dependent upon the senses solely, can never make these realities known to us. In this way is knowledge proved to be essentially different from perception.

187 B. "And now," Socrates concludes, "having wiped out all that has gone before and arrived where we now are, see if you can discern more clearly. Tell me then again what knowledge is."

"It is impossible, Socrates, to say that it is *all* opinion, since false opinion does exist; but knowledge, I think, is *true* opinion, and this shall be my answer. If, like the preceding one, it is proved incorrect, we will try to find some other."

"That is the way, Theaetetus, to answer, — boldly, not hesitatingly as before, since by taking this course we shall either find what we seek or be less likely to think we know what we really do not; and this in itself would be no contemptible gain."

Socrates now confesses himself puzzled as to the nature and origin of false opinion, and doubtful whether he had best let the whole question go, or take it up again in a new manner.

"How can you hesitate, Socrates," urges Theaetetus, "if there seems any need at all of it? Just now, in speaking about leisure, you and Theodorus said very properly that there is no pressure of haste in matters like these."

"You do right to remind me, and it is perhaps not a bad moment to go back upon our steps, for it is surely better to go over a little ground well than over much ground superficially."

The question soon arises how it can be possible to form a false opinion, if opinion be indeed the discovery of realities revealed by the mind to itself alone. While disclaiming any special knowledge on the subject, Socrates gives his own views as follows: "It seems to me," he says, "that the process of thought is nothing but a conversation where the mind asks and answers its own questions, both affirming and denying. And when, whether gradually or by sudden impulse, it has come to a decision, and unhesitatingly affirms the same, this we call its opinion. . . . And yet if we do not admit the existence of false opinion at all, we shall be forced to admit many absurdities. . . . Now if we can

191 find a way out of these and can be set free, we may then, being exempt from ridicule ourselves, afford to talk about them as other people's difficulties. But if we continue to be perplexed at every turn, we must, I suppose, humble ourselves, and let the argument trample over us like seasick passengers and do with us as it may please."

As a possible way out of the difficulty, Socrates now offers the following illustration :]

191 C. *Soc.* For the sake, then, of the argument, imagine within our souls a tablet of wax,[34] larger in one man, in another smaller, made of purer wax in one, of less pure in another, harder in some cases, softer in others, and then again something between the two.

Theaet. I have done so.

Soc. Well, let us say that this is a gift of Memory, mother of the Muses, and that whatever we may wish to remember, whether seen or heard or even imagined by us, we must stamp upon it, applying it to our perceptions and thoughts, just as if taking an impression from a seal ring. And whatever has once been impressed we remember and know as long as its image exists there; but if it gets wiped out or cannot receive the impression, we forget and do not know it. . . .

194 C. Now when the wax in the soul of a man is deep and abundant and smooth and duly tem-

pered, the impressions which come by way of the perceptions and are impressed upon this heart of the soul, as Homer calls it, alluding allegorically to its likeness to wax,[35] — these, I say, being pure and of adequate depth, are also lasting. And men of this kind have in the first place facility in learning, and in the second retentive memories; and, thirdly, they do not confuse the impressions which come from the perceptions, but have a right notion of them. For as these impressions are clear and have plenty of room, they are speedily assigned each to its own proper impress, or so called reality; and these men are called wise. Do you not agree to that?

Theaet. Most assuredly I do.

Soc. But when the heart is rough, for which the all-wise poet commends it, or when it is unclean, and the wax impure or else either excessively soft or hard, — they in whom it is soft, learn easily, but forget; if it is hard, they do the reverse; and they in whom it is rough and wild and inclined to be stony, or full of some admixture of earth or dung, have indistinct impressions. Again, when it is hard they are indistinct also, for then there is no depth; and when it is soft they are no less indistinct, because from blending together they speedily become blurred. And if besides all this, from the littleness of the soul, they are in want of room and all crowded together, they are still more indistinct than the rest.

Now all such people are subject to false opinions. When they see or hear or think of an object, they are not able to assign each thing swiftly to its own impression, but are slow about it; and because they assign wrongly they are apt to see and hear and think defectively; and of these men again we say that they are dupes, and ignorant of realities.

Theaet. Truer word was never spoken, Socrates.

Soc. May we say, then, that false opinions are within us?

Theaet. Most assuredly.

Soc. And true opinions as well?

Theaet. And true as well.

Soc. May we then assume it to be agreed that these two kinds of opinion do incontestably exist?

Theaet. Most emphatically.

Soc. What a strange and odious being, of a truth, Theaetetus, is a man who loves to talk!

Theaet. How so? Why do you say this?

Soc. Out of vexation at my own dulness and downright garrulity. For there is no other word to use when a man drags about his propositions till they get upside down, and is so stupid that he cannot be convinced, nor yet can he be made to part with a single one of his pet ideas.

Theaet. But why are you vexed at this?

Soc. Not only am I vexed, but I am uneasy as to how I shall answer if some one asks me: "Have you found out, Socrates, that false opinion consists neither in the relation of perceptions to one another, nor in that of thought, but in the union of perception and thought?" "Yes," I presume I shall answer, pluming myself, as if we had made some fine discovery.

Theaet. For my part, Socrates, I can see no reason to be ashamed of what has just been brought out.

[195 D.-197 C. Socrates now explains that the previous illustration has to do only with what is perceived by the senses, and that where some abstract idea, like that of number, is in question, another test of false and true opinion must be applied.]

197 C. *Soc.* Consider now whether it be not possible to possess knowledge and yet not have it in hand, just, for instance, as if some one had captured wild birds — doves or others — and were keeping them in a dove-cote which he had prepared for them within his own home. In one sense we might say that he always has them, seeing they are owned by him, might we not?

Theaet. Yes.

Soc. But in another sense he has not a single one of them; although he has acquired power over them, since he has them under his own control and within his own precincts, to take and to hold whenever he pleases, to capture if he likes and then let go again; all of which he may do as often as he sees fit.

Theaet. That is true.

Soc. Once more, then, just as a while ago we set up some sort of a waxen figment in the soul, so let us now fashion in each mind a kind of dove-cote filled with all manner of birds, some in flocks apart from the rest, some in small numbers, some singly and flying among the others in any chance direction.

Theaet. Regard it as done. What next?

Soc. We must assume that in childhood this is an empty receptacle, and that instead of birds there are varieties of knowledge. Now, whatever kind of knowledge a man acquires and shuts up within his precincts, we must say that he has learned or discovered the thing of which it is the knowledge, and that just this is knowing.

Theaet. So be it.

. . . .

198 D. *Soc.* Let us, then, pursuing the figure of the chase and possession of birds, say that the chase is twofold,—one before possession, for mere possession's sake; the other in order that the possessor may take and hold in his hands what he had long ago acquired. So that things which by study he had long ago learned and come to know, he can once more gain knowledge of, by resuming and holding fast the knowledge of each thing which he used to possess, but had not uppermost in his mind. . . .

199 A. But it can never happen that a man is ignorant of what he knows, although of course he

may get hold of a false opinion in regard to it. For he may have a knowledge, not of this, but of something else instead, as when, chasing them as they fly, he by mistake gets hold of one kind of knowledge in place of another; when, for instance, imagining eleven to be twelve he takes the knowledge of eleven for that of twelve, the ring-dove as it were within him instead of the pigeon.

Theaet. Yes, that is reasonable.

. . . .

Soc. Thus, then, we are rid of the notion that we do not know what we know, for it is no longer the case that we do not possess what we do possess, whether we deceive ourselves about it or not. But all the same I suspect that a still greater danger is taking shape beside us.

[199 C.–210 B. The difficulty is thus stated: how can a man seek, unless he knows what he is seeking? how, in other words, can one whose mind is filled with knowledge take anything for that which it is not?

"Perhaps," Theaetetus suggests, "we did wrong to make our birds stand for forms of knowledge only, and ought to have imagined, flying about in the soul, forms of ignorance as well; so that in regard to the same thing the pursuer would at one time get hold of a form of ignorance, at another of a form of knowledge.

"It is not easy," Socrates declares, " to abstain

from praising you. Nevertheless I must ask you to reconsider what you have said."

Examination proves the suggestion of Theaetetus to be of no avail, and it is finally agreed that before we can understand false opinion, knowledge itself must be understood. A final definition is attempted by Theaetetus, namely, —"true opinion with the addition of reason;" but this too, after an elaborate investigation, is proved untenable, and the dialogue is in the following manner brought to a close.]

210 B. *Soc.* Are we then, my friend, still in travail with knowledge, or have we brought forth everything?

Theaet. Yes, and I declare, by Zeus, that by your help I have said more than there was in me.

Soc. And yet does not this art of ours declare that all which has been brought forth is not worth rearing?

Theaet. It does decidedly.

Soc. Well, Theaetetus, if, after this experience, you should ever attempt to conceive other thoughts, they will be the better by reason of this present search; if not, you will be less exacting and more kindly to your companions, for you will have the wisdom not to think you know what you do not know. Just so much as this and no more can my art accomplish; nor do I know aught of the things that are known by the great and wondrous men who have been and are to-day. This art, however, both I and my mother have received from God, — she for women, I for fair and noble youths.

And now I must present myself at the Porch of the King,[36] to answer the indictment which Meletus has served against me. To-morrow morning, Theaetetus, let us meet here again.

NOTES.

NOTES ON CHARMIDES.

NOTE 1, p. 3.

In the *Symposium* Alcibiades speaks of the fortitude displayed by Socrates during the expedition to POTIDAEA (432–429 B. C.), of his indifference to cold and hunger, and of his coolness and courage in battle.

NOTE 2, p. 3.

The TEMPLE or sacred enclosure here referred to was, until recently, supposed to be that adjacent to the King's Porch (see Note 36 on *Theaetetus*), the text being altered from βασίλης to βασιλικῆς to suit this meaning.

The recent discovery of an inscription mentioning land sacred to BASILE has established the fact that there was a goddess or other sacred person of this name, though whether or not she was identical with Basileia, worshipped as the personification of royalty, it is impossible to determine. Equally uncertain is it whether the word here translated *temple* refers to a building or merely to a sacred precinct, — perhaps the same described in the inscription as lying on the southern outskirts of the city, and about to be planted with two hundred olive-trees and leased to a tenant.

NOTE 3, p. 3.

This is the same CHAEREPHON of whom Socrates says in the *Apology:* "You know, of course, what sort of man he was, and how eager in whatever he undertook. Well, once he went to Delphi, and had the boldness to consult the oracle on this matter, and to ask if any one were wiser than I." — *Apol.* 21 A.

NOTE 4, p. 4.

Critias, a near connection of Plato and a poet and orator, was perhaps the author of the treatise *On the Athenian State* (ascribed falsely to Xenophon), which is the earliest fragment extant of Attic prose. He is here represented in a more favourable light than in history, where he appears as the greediest and most bloodthirsty of the detested Thirty Tyrants.

NOTE 5, p. 5.

CHARMIDES, who was the maternal uncle of Plato, is said to have shown in private debate extraordinary fitness for the career of a statesman, but to have been prevented, by want of self-confidence, from taking any part in the popular assemblies. (Xen. *Mem.* iii. 7.) It has been conjectured that Plato, to whose aristocratic mind such abstinence doubtless appeared more than excusable, introduced him into this dialogue with a view to removing any unfavourable impression of him that may have existed. While praising the youth for the modesty so becoming to his years, he does not fail to point out the real dignity which underlies his character and the humour which enlivens it. Charmides was afterward one of the Ten who governed in Peiraeus under the Thirty Tyrants. He and Critias were both killed in the battle at Munychia, fighting against Thrasybulus and the democratic party.

NOTE 6, p. 5.

That among the Greeks personal beauty was measured by the form even more than by the face is clearly shown by Chaerephon's subsequent words, even if it were not sufficiently proved by the excellence of Greek statuary.

The almost reverential admiration excited by beauty is well illustrated by the attitude of these young boys, as it is by the talk of the Trojan graybeards in the Iliad, who, as they watch Helen's approach, whisper to each other, —

> "Small blame is theirs, if both the Trojan knights
> And brazen-mailed Achaians have endured
> So long so many evils for the sake
> Of that one woman. She is wholly like
> In feature to the deathless goddesses."
>
> *Iliad*, iii. 154-158 (Bryant's translation).

NOTE 7, p. 6.

The words here translated "perfection itself" soon lost their literal signification of "beautiful and good," and came to mean "an accomplished gentleman." In this sense καλὸς κἀγαθός was frequently applied to the upper classes, as in Plato's *Republic* (viii. 569 A.), where the aristocrats are spoken of as "those who are called rich and beautiful and good."

NOTE 8, p. 6.

Several fragments of SOLON's poems still exist, relating chiefly to his political and legislative activity. His intention of making a version in hexameter of his laws is mentioned in the *Life of Solon* by Plutarch, who gives what purport to be the first lines of this version.

This allusion to Solon, and the praise bestowed afterward upon the ancestors of Charmides, seem to show that Plato, who was nephew to Charmides, was not without pride of family.

NOTE 9, p. 8.

The use of charms as healing agents, in earlier days very prevalent among the Greeks, was, even in the fifth century, by no means confined to the ignorant classes. It is therefore quite in keeping with his assumed character that Socrates professes to have a charm for the cure of headache. Only as the conversation progresses does he lay aside the character of physician and healer, and allow it to become evident that he refers not to magic words or incantations, but to some subtler charm, such as the "songs which have power to charm young men into virtue" (*Laws*, 671 A.), or the influence of the "potent charmer" who can "charm away the fears of the child within us," that he may no longer "dread death as a bugbear."— *Phaedo*, 77 E.

NOTE 10, p. 9.

Herodotus reports a story that ZAMOLXIS acquired his wisdom from Pythagoras, whose slave he was, and that on his return to Thrace he practised the healing art among his own people with such success that he was honoured as a god. The legend that he conferred immortality is easily accounted for by his having taught the doctrine of a future life.

This whole passage is curiously in harmony with the mind-healing theory of to-day.

NOTE 11, p. 11.

Plato's definition of TEMPERANCE, it need hardly be said, includes far more than the common definition of this virtue. Σωφροσύνη, or temperance,—a quality which embraces soundness of mind, good sense, moderation, and various other virtues, including wisdom itself,—is defined in the *Republic* (iv. 442 C.-D.) as the submission of the soul's impulses and desires to the rule of reason, inducing thereby harmony within the soul itself.

In the *Gorgias* we are told that the temperate man is one who "will fulfil his duties toward gods and men, . . . his dealings in relation to men being just, toward the gods reverent, . . . and he will, moreover, be courageous, . . . and, being just and courageous and holy, he must needs be perfectly good, and he who is good does well and nobly all that he does; and he who does well fares well and is blessed and happy."—*Gorg.* 507 A.-D.

NOTE 12, p. 12.

ABARIS was a celebrated Thracian sage, who is said once to have delivered the earth from a plague, and about whom various fabulous stories are told, such as that he lived without food.

NOTE 13, p. 13.

"Shame ill becomes a beggar-man."
Odyss. xvii. 347.

This line is also quoted in the *Laches*, 201 A.

NOTE 14, p. 16.

PRODICUS is always spoken of by Plato in a tone of good-natured raillery. In the *Laches* he is said to be of all the Sophists "the best at pulling words to pieces," and in the Protagoras an amusing account is given of the man and his ways. He is chiefly known by the fable of the Choice of Herakles preserved to us by Xenophon — *Mem.* ii. 1, 21.

NOTE 15, p. 17.

Plato elsewhere alludes to the hoped-for advent of some great and, perhaps, superhuman master, whose judgment on all subjects is to be final. In the *Phaedo* (77 E.) we are told that diligent search must be made for a "potent charmer" who shall charm away the fear of death, as in *Laches* (196 A.) it is hinted that he "who has a knowledge of what is or is not to be feared" may prove to be a god.

NOTE 16, p. 18.

This declaration in regard to self-knowledge is in direct opposition to the views expressed by Socrates in all the other Platonic dialogues. But formal consistency with his own writings was no part of Plato's plan, his aim being to carry each separate point of view to its extreme conclusion, without reference to the opinions which he has elsewhere set forth.

NOTE 17, p. 18.

When, in the Cratylus, an attempt is made to discover the origin of words, the idea that they were imposed by some ancient legislator is rejected, for the reason that "it is impossible to know things save either by being taught their names or by finding them out;" whereupon Cratylus suggests that some power greater than human assigned to all things their first names. — *Crat.* 438 B.-C.

NOTES ON LYSIS.

NOTE 1, p. 23.

The ACADEMY, where Plato afterward taught, was about a mile north of the city, the road thither being lined on either side with the tombs of the most illustrious Athenians. Outside the city in a different direction was the Lyceum, thus named in honour of Apollo Lyceus, or the wolf-god, to whom it was dedicated. Here is laid the scene of the *Theaetetus*, and here in after days came Aristotle with his followers. Spacious gardens were attached to both these gymnasiums, the stream to which the FOUNTAIN OF PANOPS gave birth flowing through that of the Lyceum. This fountain, or spring, is casually mentioned by Hesychius, as follows: "Panops is an Attic hero. There is of him a temple and a statue and a spring."

NOTE 2, p. 23.

Here, as in the *Euthydemus*, CTESIPPUS is represented as a rollicking, somewhat bumptious fellow, full of high spirits and fun. That he formed one of the Socratic circle is evident from his presence at the death of Socrates. (See *Phaedo*, 59, C.) Nothing further is known of the other characters here named.

NOTE 3, p. 25.

As Hermes was the god who presided over the gymnasium and palaestrum, Athenian boys celebrated his festival (the Hermaea) in these resorts, where, after offering sacrifices, they were allowed to play games and amuse themselves freely.

MENEXENUS, whose name occurs just below, is frequently mentioned by Plato, one of whose dialogues bears his name. We hear of him in the *Phaedo* as one of the friends present at the death of Socrates.

Note 4, p. 25.

In this room, which was called the Apodyterium, were left the garments of those who were bathing or exercising. The gymnastic exercises probably took place in the large oblong court, which was the principal feature of the palaestrae or gymnasia. It was surrounded by a colonnade, a double row of pillars on one side forming a spacious portico, out of which led various apartments for the use of bathers.

In the court and porticos were seats, and here the philosophers and teachers were in the habit of collecting their listeners around them.

Note 5, p. 30.

The plectrum was a little stick or wand used for striking the lyre.

Note 6, p. 34.

This seems to have been a favourite oath with Socrates, and has been thought to refer to the dog-headed Anubis, the Egyptian Hermes.

Note 7, p. 37.

The care of a Greek boy after the age of six or seven devolved upon an attendant or pedagogue. It was his duty, not to teach but to have general charge of his young master, accompanying him to school and elsewhere, and often carrying his books for him. Although the pedagogue was always a slave, so responsible a position was supposed to be occupied by one, if not of education, at least of character and refinement. That this, however, was not universally the case, is evident from a passage in Plutarch: "Of those slaves who are capable they appoint some as husbandmen, some as skippers, some as traders, some as stewards, some as money-lenders; but whenever they find some drunken, greedy fellow, of no use for any kind of work, they turn the boys over to him." — Plut., *de lib. educ.* 7.

NOTES ON LACHES.

Note 1, p. 41.

Those who taught the art of fighting in armour and the use of weapons were accustomed, after the manner of the Sophists, to give exhibitions of their skill, with the view of attracting pupils.

Freedom of movement with courage and coolness in action are among the advantages enumerated by Nicias, in the course of the dialogue, as derived from proficiency in this kind of combat.

Note 2, p. 41.

The THUCYDIDES here mentioned is not the historian, but the politician who, being the rival of Pericles for supremacy in the State, was ostracized in 444 B.C. The father of Lysimachus was ARISTIDES the Just, whose reputation for "justice," was such that he was chosen by the allies to assess the sum which each member of the confederacy of Delos was to pay into the common treasury.

In *Meno* (94 A.D.) the insignificant characters of LYSIMACHUS and MELESIAS are held up as a proof that virtue cannot be taught, since, had it been possible to impart it, like gymnastics or any other branch of education, their fathers would have "found out some one who would have made good men of them."

Note 3, p. 44.

At the time when the enemies of Pericles were beginning to attack him through his friends, DAMON and Anaxagoras were compelled to leave Athens, because, as former teachers of Pericles, they had always remained on terms of intimacy with him.

Note 4, p. 45.

Socrates' behaviour during this retreat is thus described by Alcibiades, rather to the disadvantage of his present panegyrist: "I observed how far superior he was to Laches in presence of mind, for he then appeared just as you have described him, stalking about there as he does here to-day, his head erect, and casting his eyes around, and calmly scrutinizing friend and foe. It was plain to see, even from a distance, that if any one were to lay hands upon this man, he would stoutly defend himself." — *Symp.* 221 B.

Note 5, p. 46.

The parallel here drawn between Athens and Lacedaemon is hardly supported by facts. The Lacedaemonians were opposed to all changes, in education as in other things. So the Sophist Hippias (*Hippias Major*, 283) declares that in spite of his numerous visits to Sparta he has never made any money in that city by his teaching, and adds that "it is not lawful among them to introduce a foreign mode of education" (*Ibid.* 284).

Athens, on the other hand, with her wealth and prosperity and the stimulus imparted to the arts by the refined taste of Pericles, became not only the commercial capital of Greece, but the chief centre of the artistic and literary world. Whoever had anything to exhibit naturally found his way to the city, where constant opportunity for seeing and hearing masterpieces had produced the most accomplished critics of antiquity, and where at certain seasons all Greece was assembled as audience.

Note 6, p. 47.

LACHES was, with Charoeades, commander of the twenty ships sent to Sicily in 427 B. C. by the Athenians to assist the Leontines against the Syracusans. It may have been in the course of this expedition that he saw Stesilaus under the trying circumstances described in the text. Laches was relieved of his command after a little more than a year, but appears again in 418 B. C. as one of the commanders of the Athenian contingent in the battle of Mantinea, where he lost his life.

NOTE 7, p. 48.

The poverty of Socrates is pleaded upon a more important occasion, when in suggesting the penalty of a fine, he remarks: "But in my case that will be neither more nor less than imprisonment, for I have no money wherewith to pay it." — *Apol.* 37 C.

NOTE 8, p. 49.

In Greece the religious element was never wanting in any concern of daily life. Thus, although the division of Attica into demes or townships was originally made for political reasons solely, each deme had from the first its own peculiar celebrations and observances, and its inhabitants were united by religious no less than by secular bonds.

NOTE 9, p. 49.

Compare this with the account put into the mouth of Alcibiades (*Symp.* 216 A.). "Often," he says, " I have been brought to such a state by this Marsyas that it has seemed to me impossible to live as I am. . . . For he compels me to acknowledge that I am greatly at fault in that, while busying myself about the interests of the Athenians, I am neglecting my own soul. . . . Therefore, stopping my ears as if to shut out the voice of sirens, I tear myself away by force, lest I grow old sitting at his feet."

NOTE 10, p. 49.

Plutarch quotes Solon as saying that he —

"Each day grew older and learnt something new."

The subsequent career of Nicias proved that, in his case at least, old age did not bring with it wisdom. He was a man whose sterling integrity and dignity of character had raised him deservedly to posts of highest honour; but the irresolution and timidity which grew upon him with increasing years cost his country, in the fateful expedition against Syracuse, a shameful defeat, and sent him to an unhonoured grave.

Note 11, p. 50.

The ancients recognized seven, if not more scales or kinds of music, differing from each other not simply in pitch but in quality, somewhat as do the minor and major keys of modern music. Plato (*Rep.* III. 398 C.–399 E.) discusses several of these varieties. He excludes from his ideal republic the Ionian and Lydian, on the ground that they are soft and adapted to drinking-songs, but admits the Phrygian and Dorian, since they encourage fortitude and endurance in dangers, and self-restraint and moderation in good fortune.

> " Anon they move
> In perfect phalanx to the Dorian mood
> Of flutes and soft recorders; such as raised
> To height of noblest temper heroes old
> Arming to battle.
> Milton, *Par. Lost*, i. 550.

Note 12, p. 55.

See Note 15 on *Charmides* for other allusions to the advent of one whose knowledge will exceed that now possessed by any mortal.

Note 13, p. 56.

Plutarch tells us that, in spite of his advanced age, LAMACHUS, who, with Nicias, was a leader in the expedition against Syracuse, displayed a courage and intrepidity worthy of an Alcibiades.

The citizens of the deme of AEXONE, to which Laches belonged, were noted for their abusiveness of speech.

Note 14, p. 58.

NICERATUS afterwards perished at the hands of the Thirty Tyrants.

NOTES ON EUTHYDEMUS.

NOTE 1, p. 63.

CLEINIAS, the son of Axiochus, is not named in any other Platonic dialogue, except casually in the spurious *Axiochus*, where he summons Socrates to the deathbed of his father.

CRITOBULUS, the son of Crito, is casually mentioned elsewhere.

NOTE 2, p. 63.

EUTHYDEMUS is not to be confounded with his namesake of Xenophon's *Memorabilia*, an accomplished youth who profited by the searching cross-examination of Socrates. That the man and his teachings were widely known is evident from a passage in the *Cratylus*, where his name follows that of Protagoras. "You do not believe with Euthydemus," Socrates there declares, "that all men possess all things equally at the same time and always; for in that case, and if virtue and vice were possessed equally by all, some would not, as is actually the case, be bad, and others good." — *Crat.* 386 D.

DIONYSODORUS is known only as the helpmeet of his brother, although the ingenious hypothesis of a German writer (Teichmüller) identifies him with the orator Lysias, who is mentioned in the *Republic* as son of the aged Cephalus and brother of Euthydemus and Polemarchus.

NOTE 3, p. 64.

THURII was an Italian colony of Athens, which maintained close relations with the mother-country.

We seem to read here between the lines a sly suspicion that this exile was due not simply to political reasons, but in part to the odium in which the Sophists were held by their own countrymen.

Note 4, p. 64.

This passing hit at the practice of receiving pay for instruction is in keeping with the views of both Socrates and Plato upon the subject.

The PANCRATIAST was a professional athlete who devoted himself to feats of strength, such as boxing and wrestling, to the exclusion of other gymnastic exercises, thus developing to an abnormal degree certain parts of the body, sometimes at the expense of his general health.

The inhabitants of ACARNANIA, one of the outlying districts of Greece, were noted for their skill in the use of the sling and other arts of warfare, and were consequently in great demand as mercenary troops. The brothers mentioned in the text, although they had evidently attained some contemporary celebrity, are not known to fame.

Note 5, p. 66.

The familiar sign or daemon seems in this instance, as in so many others, to have been a presentiment which "made itself heard," as Socrates says (*Apol.* 31 D.-E.), "only to turn me back from what I am about to do, but never to impel me forward."

Note 6, p. 66.

PAEANIA was the same deme of Attica to which Demosthenes the orator belonged. See Note 2 on *Lysis* for further mention of Ctesippus.

Note 7, p. 67.

The teaching of virtue, which Protagoras proclaimed to be the true end of his art, is attempted merely in name by these less respectable Sophists, who seem to have adopted the doctrines of the Eleatic philosophers only to employ them in paradoxical quibbles.

Note 8, p. 72.

Aristotle, in his treatise on *Fallacies*, was the first to analyze and classify verbal puzzles of this kind.

A well known author has aptly remarked that even in our own day "a sophism, perfectly analogous in character to those which Plato here exposes to ridicule, may, in another case, easily escape detection from the hearer, and even from the reasoner himself. People are constantly misled by fallacies arising from the same word bearing two senses. . . . If these fallacies appear so obviously inconclusive that they can deceive no one, the reason lies not in the premises themselves, but in the particular conclusions to which they lead; which conclusions are known on other grounds to be false, and never to be seriously maintained by any person." — Grote's *Plato*, vol. i. p. 549.

Note 9, p. 75.

The wild music and dances in honour of Cybele were encouraged and shared by the CORYBANTES, the name by which the priests of this goddess in Phrygia were known.

In the rites of initiation games and other frolics played a part, as is the case in many secret societies of to-day.

Note 10, p. 79.

The bare suggestion of wishing a friend's destruction is supposed to convey with it an evil omen which Ctesippus would fain have transferred from his own head to that of the evil wisher.

Note 11, p. 80.

The Cappadocians, Cretans, and Carians, owing to their unenviable reputation for faithlessness, were known as the three bad kappas, their common initial letter; the Carians especially being regarded as the lowest dregs of the population and treated no better than dogs. The name of ÇARIAN, and of

Thracian as well, was synonymous with that of slave, probably because most of the Greek slaves came from those provinces.

The allusion below is to the story of Medea, who having, by process of boiling, turned an old ram into a lamb, persuaded the daughters of Pelias to cut their father in pieces and boil him, under the pretence that he would thus be restored to youth.

Further on the story of MARSYAS is referred to, — the Phrygian satyr, who, having picked up the discarded flute of Athene and finding that of itself it emitted beautiful sounds, presumed to challenge Apollo and his cithara. On being adjudged by the Muses the inferior of Apollo, he was flayed alive and his skin suspended in the cave where rose the river of which he was the god. The character of the satyr makes the use of his skin for a wine-jar peculiarly appropriate.

The tale is doubtless a fabled account of the rival claims of cithara and flute; the former being used in the worship of Apollo, the other in that of Cybele.

NOTE 12, p. 81.

PROTEUS, the sea-god, who assumed all sorts of shapes to avoid being forced to disclose his knowledge (Hom. *Od.* iv. 384 foll.), is no unfitting prototype of teachers who took every opportunity to throw their adversary off the track by quibbles, each more absurd than the last. Whoever wished to obtain an answer from Proteus was obliged to hold him fast until he returned to his proper form, a feat said to have been accomplished by Menelaus.

This same Proteus is portrayed by Euripides (*Helena*) as king of Egypt, at whose court rather than at that of King Priam of Troy, he supposes Helen to have tarried.

NOTE 13, p. 83.

His own supposed want of memory was a standing joke with Socrates himself. "It so happens," he declares, "that I am a forgetful man, and if any one talks to me at length I quite lose track of the subject." — *Prot.* 334 C.

Note 14, p. 84.

The electric lights called by modern sailors St. Elmo's fire were regarded by the ancients as manifestations of the Dioscuri, — otherwise known as the twin brothers Castor and Pollux, — who were supposed to care for mariners and travellers generally. Hence Socrates, in danger from the waves of discussion, thinks of the Dioscuri, whom he would naturally invoke if exposed to a tempestuous sea. The expression "triple wave" refers to a notion current among the Greeks that every third wave was greater than its two predecessors. "You do not seem aware that when I have barely escaped the first and second waves, you are now bringing upon me the third and most terrible one of all." — *Rep.* 472 A.

Note 15, p. 87.

The Lernean HYDRA was slain by Heracles, with the aid of his nephew Iolaus. That the newly arrived monster should be described as bearing down from the left makes the allusion to Dionysodorus, who was seated at the left of Socrates, seem more pointed.

Of PATROCLES, the nephew of Socrates, little or nothing further is known.

Note 16, p. 89.

The epithet "ancestral" was given by the ancients to the deity from whom they derived their origin. Zeus was worshipped in some cities as the ancestral deity, and, according to the Scholiast on Aristophanes' *Clouds* (1468), bore this epithet also in Athens, though Socrates here seems to say that he was worshipped in Athens only as a god of the family and of the phratry or tribal division.

Note 17, p. 92.

These words are found in the opening of the first and the close of the third Olympian odes.

Note 18, p. 92.

We may detect here a good-natured rallying of Crito upon his well known love of acquisition.

Note 19, p. 94.

This description is supposed to refer to ISOCRATES, a rhetorical teacher, political essayist, and writer of speeches to be spoken in the courts of justice. In his youth he was a pupil of Socrates, but thought he derived little benefit from the pursuit of philosophy. He seems, in Plato's opinion, to have resembled the "four," spoken of in the *Gorgias*, who, "banded together in the quest of wisdom," exhorted one another to "take care lest, by becoming over-wise, they should unwittingly work their own ruin."—*Gorg.* 487 C.

Yet in the *Phaedrus* Plato speaks in no unflattering terms of Isocrates, who was not only a friend of kings and a teacher of teachers, but was also the founder of an important branch of literary prose. His death is said to have been caused by the report of the fatal battle which made Philip of Macedonia master of Greece.

" As that dishonest victory
At Chaeronea, fatal to liberty,
Killed with report that old man eloquent."
Milton, *Sonnet X.*

NOTES ON THEAETETUS.

NOTE 1, p. 99.

The Agora was not only the centre of civic politics and the chief place for the transaction of business, but the public promenade where at certain hours all the world was to be found. In the *Gorgias* (485 D.) the philosopher is censured by the worldly Callicles because he "avoids the heart of the city and the Agora, where, as the poet tells us, men acquire eminence."

EUCLID of Megara must not be confounded with the celebrated mathematician of the same name. That he was an ardent follower of Socrates is shown by the story of his nightly visits to him, in woman's disguise, at a time when the Megarians were forbidden under pain of death to visit Athens. After the death of Socrates, he founded in Megara a school which combined the Eleatic philosophy, familiar to him from youth, with the dialectics and ethical teachings of his master.

NOTE 2, p. 99.

Of the many engagements which took place at CORINTH, that of 394 B. C., when the Athenians and their allies were severely defeated by the Lacedaemonians, is probably referred to in the text. A peculiar interest is lent to this battle by the beautiful monument to the young knight Dexileos, with its inscription: "One of the five horsemen who perished at Corinth in the archonship of Eubulides."

NOTE 3, p. 101.

ERINEUM, a town near Eleusis, on the road from Megara to Athens, was said to be the spot where Pluto descended to Hades with Persephone. — Paus. I. 38, 5.

Note 4, p. 101.

Here a break occurs, the conversation being resumed within the house of Euclid.

The change from the narrative to the dramatic form has been held by some writers to determine the chronological order of Plato's dialogues, those which are narrative being presumably earlier than the *Theaetetus*, those which are dramatic of later date.

This dialogue is the only one supposed to be read from the notes of a person who had taken no part in it.

There is a passage in the so-called letters of Xenophon from which we gather that, although Plato undoubtedly borrowed from the transcript of Euclid, so much was added of his own invention that the original was no longer to be recognized.

Note 5, p. 101.

THEODORUS of Cyrene, a former pupil of Protagoras, was a celebrated mathematician and geometrician, with whom Plato is said to have studied. He is not to be confounded with the later Cyrenaic philosopher, Theodorus the Atheist.

Note 6, p. 102.

In the *Symposium* (215-217) Socrates is compared by Alcibiades to the masks of Silenus and also to Marsyas the Satyr.

Those passages and that of the text are the principal descriptions given by Plato of the personal appearance of Socrates.

Note 7, p. 103.

The rare union of the qualities held by Plato to be the peculiar property of the philosopher is elsewhere spoken of: "How," he asks, "shall we find a nature that is at once gentle and high-spirited? For gentleness of nature seems to be at variance with high spirit." — *Repub.* 375 C.

NOTE 8, p. 103.

The only one of these " companions " subsequently mentioned is Socrates the younger (147 C.).

From the allusion to a race-course and to the anointing of the youths, the scene is evidently a gymnasium, probably the Lyceum. See the *Euthyphro*, which in point of time is the sequence of this dialogue. " What new thing has happened, Socrates," it is there asked, " that you have left the Lyceum and come here to the Porch of the King ? " And compare the closing words of the *Theaetetus:* " And now I must take my way to the Porch of the King to answer the indictment which Miletus has served against me."

NOTE 9, p. 104.

The rather peremptory mode of address and the use of the vocative bespeak the relationship of master and pupil.

The deme to which EUPHRONIUS, the father of Theaetetus, belonged was in Attica, so that he was accounted an Athenian, although his residence was not within the city.

NOTE 10, p. 108.

The effect produced by Socrates upon his hearers is described in the *Meno*, 80 A.-B. : " Both in outward form and in your effect upon others, you seem to me, if I may be allowed a jest, very like the flat torpedo fish, who renders torpid those that come near and lay hold of him. Even so you seem now to have done to me, for my soul and my speech are in fact torpid, so that I am not able to answer you. Thousands of times ere now and to many people have I said all manner of things about virtue, — and very well too, I thought ; but now I cannot even say what virtue is."

NOTE 11, p. 110.

The full meaning of what Plato calls perception or sense-knowledge is better conveyed by the German " Wahrnehmung " than by any one English word, and its comprehensiveness is shown by a sentence which occurs later in the dialogue —

"The senses have sundry names, — those of sight, hearing, smelling, and likewise those of cold, heat, and pleasures, pains, desires, and fears." — *Theaet.* 156 B.

NOTE 12, p. 110.

PROTAGORAS, the celebrated philosopher of Abdera, nicknamed "the All-Wise," is chiefly known to us by the maxim, "Man is the measure of all things," of which the following is an amplified form: "As things appear to me, so they are to me; as they appear to you, so to you; for you are a man, and so am I." — *Theaet.* 152 A. Plato, although he often misinterprets the doctrines of Protagoras and, as in this dialogue, "runs him hard," evidently holds him in affectionate regard. In his dialogue of the *Protagoras*, he not only makes him the mouthpiece of admirable views on punishment and education, but gives him a certain advantage in the discussion.

HERACLITUS of Ephesus, sometimes called the "weeping philosopher," who maintained the doctrine of universal motion, should not be held responsible for the loose and sceptical views which his followers adopted after his death, and which are treated with such contempt by Theodorus (180 A.–B.).

EMPEDOCLES of Agrigentum, whom Aristotle calls a "Homeric spirit," was a poet and statesman as well as philosopher. A disciple of Parmenides, he soon departed from the Eleatic doctrine of unity and fixedness, and taught that fire, air, water, and earth are the fundamental principles of all things.

NOTE 13, p. 111.

Eurip. *Hippolytus*, 612 : "My tongue has sworn, but my mind is unsworn." This passage is referred to several times by Plato, and also by Aristophanes and Cicero.

NOTE 14, p. 111.

The personification of Divine Philosophy in IRIS may have been suggested by the parentage of this messenger of the gods.

"Electra, the daughter of deep-flowing ocean, did Thaumas espouse, and to Iris, swift-footed, gave birth." — Hes. *Theog*. 265.

"By wondering (θαυμαζειν)," says Aristotle, "men now as in olden days begin the study of philosophy;" and he stated further that philosophy ceases with the cessation of wonder. — *Metaph. I.* A similar doctrine was taught by Democritus and by the Stoics.

NOTE 15, p. 112.

Those who were initiated into the sacred mysteries were believed to possess truths handed down by tradition from distant ages. Plato, therefore, calls such as content themselves with "that which lies nearest them" and is perceived by the senses the "uninitiated." These are the materialists described in the *Sophist* (246 A.-B.) as men who "maintain that only what may be touched and handled has real existence, because they define soul and body as one and the same; and they will not hear of anything different, but if any one asserts that aught can exist without a body they utterly despise him."

In comparison with these, Protagoras is an idealist. He held that, since all things are relative, it can hardly be said that a thing is, but rather that it is ever coming into being through its relation to some other thing. The same, he maintained, is true of qualities: they are the product of two kinds of motion, one of which is active and proceeds from the subject, while the other is passive and proceeds from the object of perception. Thus colour may be explained as the product of motion, proceeding on the one hand from the eye, and on the other from the object which appears to possess colour. By some such hidden process is that which we call "appearance" caused.

NOTE 16, p. 119.

From this passage and that of 162 A., it may be inferred that the Lacedaemonians allowed none to enter their gymnasiums who would not take part in the exercises.

SCIRON was a robber, who, as the story goes, compelled the

travellers whom he had robbed to wash his feet, and then hurled them down from the top of a high rock which stood near the frontier of Megara. He met his reward at the hands of Theseus; but, the earth refusing to receive him, he was suspended mid-air, and finally changed into a rock in commemoration of his past misdeeds.

ANTAEUS, the Lydian giant, son of Poseidon and Earth, compelled all whom he met to wrestle with him, gaining, himself, fresh strength from every contact with Earth, his mother. It was only by lifting him from the ground that Heracles was finally able to vanquish and slay him.

NOTE 17, p. 121.

The image of the old philosopher suddenly raising up his head and as suddenly disappearing again may have been suggested by "Charon's steps," a flight of stairs used in the theatre for introducing ghosts upon the scene.

A covert sarcasm may here be intended on the well known unwillingness of Protagoras to listen to the statements made by his opponents.

NOTE 18, p. 121.

It is interesting to compare this remark with the statement of Socrates that "at the age of more than seventy years, I am now for the first time appearing before a court of justice, so that I am an utter stranger to the manner of speaking there." —*Apol.* 17 D.

See also the *Gorgias* (486 B.), where Callicles asserts that Socrates, if made to appear before a court, would stand "dizzy and gaping, and with never a word to say."

NOTE 19, p. 122.

The rule that nothing outside of the subject-matter might be touched upon was not strictly observed, as appears from an allusion in the *Apology* to the defendant turning suppliant (*Apol.* 34 C.).

The expression rendered, "the so-called affidavits," refers to one of the first steps in an Athenian legal procedure, wherein each party in a suit made oath to the justice of his cause. Many scholars regard this as an interpolation.

The "master" just below mentioned is probably the Demus, or sovereign people, represented in the court by the presiding officer. The personification of the people was familiar to the Athenians of Plato's time from various examples, notably that in the *Knights* of Aristophanes. From the significant language here used, it would seem that Plato had some particular case in mind, very probably the trial of Socrates.

The "clepsydra," or water-clock, was always placed in full view of the orator. It consisted of a globe with a short neck for the introduction of the water, small holes being pierced on the bottom for its escape. As the length of time necessary for this process varied with the temperature, the gauge was far from a perfect one.

If this dialogue was written or finished after Plato's return from Sicily, it is possible that the whole passage may refer to the tyrant Dionysius and his habit of presiding in court, in which case the description of the sycophant which follows may apply to the historian Philistius, whose machinations nearly caused Plato's destruction. But as the dialogue is supposed to have occurred just before the trial of Socrates (see the closing sentence), it is more natural to see here a prophetic allusion to that event.

NOTE 20, p. 123.

The first recorded victory in a contest of tragedy was won by Thespis in 536. From this time dramatic and dithyrambic choral performances held in honour of the god Dionysus formed a regular part of the two great yearly festivals, and always bore the character of a contest. The chief cost, that of the choruses, was defrayed by some wealthy citizens who, under the title of choragus, received and dedicated the crown or the prize, usually a tripod, which was awarded by the judges to the victorious chorus.

NOTE 21, p. 124.

Here Plato may have had in mind the contemptible action of the rhetorician Lysias, in bringing up at the trial of the younger Alcibiades all the sins of the father, and laying them upon the son.

NOTE 22, p. 124.

A passage in the *Republic* (500 B.-C.) emphasizes the indifference of the true philosopher to worldly considerations and interests. "Is not," it is asked, "the bitterness which many feel toward philosophy due to the outsiders who, like disorderly revellers, enter in there where they do not belong, abusing and wrangling with each other, and forever talking of people, a theme which least of all befits philosophy? . . . For he whose thoughts are truly fixed upon realities has not the leisure to look downwards upon the affairs of men, nor in the struggle against them to become filled with envy and ill-will; but, from beholding and contemplating principles which are fixed and immovable and which neither injure nor are injured by each other but act always in accordance with reason and order, he imitates these and, so far as he is able, grows into their likeness."

After the usual fashion of Plato, the quotation from Pindar given a few lines above is freely interwoven into his text.

NOTE 23, p. 124.

Chaucer, in "The Milleres Tale," 3458-60, uses a similar illustration.

> "He walked in the feldes for to prie
> Upon the starres, what ther sholde befalle
> Til he was in a marle-pit y-falle."

THALES, one of the seven wise men, a native of Miletus in Ionia, is one of those to whom the maxim written on the Temple of Apollo at Delphi, "Know thyself," has been ascribed. He was not only the earliest of the Greek philosophers (born probably 624 B. C.), but the founder also of geometry and astronomy, and is thought to have predicted the eclipse of the sun which occurred in 585 B. C. According to his theory of the universe, water was the origin of all things and the life-giving element.

It has been conjectured that the "Thracian handmaid" represents Antisthenes, the founder or precursor of the Cynics, whose contempt of culture, and even of knowledge, was in Plato's eyes "slavish." The epithets applied to the handmaid are not ill suited to this philosopher, whose reputation was that of a gay and charming companion.

NOTE 24, p. 127.

An Athenian dramatist of the fourth century seems to have borrowed from this passage, in the lines of which the following is a literal translation: —

"Family is my despair. If you love me, mother, speak not about each man's family. They who have nothing good in their own nature straightway fly to the tombs, and begin to count over the number of their ancestors. But they gain naught thereby, nor can you mention one who has no ancestors; how else, indeed, were he born?" — Menander, *Fragm.* 533.

If Plato's real opinion is expressed in the words of the text, his well known bias in favour of aristocracy would seem to have proceeded not from belief in the intrinsic value of good birth, but from a conviction that it is true of inherited position as it is of inherited fortune that they who have received it "do not care over-much for it," while "they who have made their own fortune (or position) value it as their own work, besides valuing it for its uses, as the others do." (*Repub.* 330 C.) He accepted aristocracy in its literal meaning, — the rule of *the best*, that "small remnant of true philosophers" (*Repub.* 496 B.), whose leadership if followed would ensure the fulfilment of justice, and who alone are capable of mastering political science, of all sciences the most difficult (see *Laws*, 864 A.).

It is reported of Socrates that, on hearing Alcibiades boast of his lands and possessions, he showed the youth a map of the world, bidding him point them out upon it.

NOTE 25, p. 128.

The same idea is found in the allegory of the Cave (*Repub.* 515 E.-516 A.). "If any one were to draw him by force up the steep narrow way, and not let go of him till he had drawn him into the sunlight, would he not suffer and be in distress; and after he had come to the light, and his eyes were full of it, would he not be unable to behold any one of those things that are called truth?"

NOTE 26, p. 128.

The cloak was a large oblong cloth first thrown over the left shoulder and passed round the back to the right side, and then over the right arm, to be finally brought again over the left shoulder. According to a man's skill or awkwardness in wearing this garment he was held to be a gentleman or a boor.

As it was customary for travellers to carry their own bedding, it formed a chief part of the equipment needed for a journey, and thus the term just above translated by this word came to be applied to luggage in general.

In contrast to the "flattering speech" of the slave, see the description in *Laches* (188 D.) of the "harmonious language," the use of which marks the true freeman.

NOTE 27, p. 128.

Many passages in Plato's writings, like that of the text, describe holiness as perfected only through union with the divine.

"In their search to discover within themselves the nature of God they have the less difficulty, because they have been compelled to gaze steadfastly upon him; thus their memory clings to him, and they become inspired, and derive his character and his ways, so far as it is possible for man to partake of the nature of God. — *Phaedrus*, 253 A.

"Rightly does the mind of the philosopher alone have wings; for he, so far as may be, keeps ever before him the memory of those things in virtue of which even God himself is divine. Therefore a man who uses aright such memories as these is forever being initiated into perfect mysteries, and alone attains the mystery of perfection." —*Phaedrus*, 249 C.

"By constant intercourse with the steadfast and the divine he himself becomes divine and steadfast, so far as is possible to man."— *Repub.* 500 D.

NOTE 28, p. 129.

"He who is really fighting for the right," Socrates elsewhere declares, "must, if he would be safe even for a short time, lead a private life, not a public one." — *Apol.* 32 A.

The words "cumbering the ground," cited also in the *Apology* (28 D.), are carelessly quoted from the speech of Achilles to Thetis his mother. — Hom. *Il.* 18, 104.

NOTE 29, p. 130.

See the *Phaedo*, where the future of a spiritual nature is contrasted with that of an earthly one.

"When then the soul departs in this state, she goes to the world which is invisible like herself, to the world divine and immortal and full of thought; there, set free from error, folly, fears, and the fierce passions and other ills of humanity, her lot is a happy one indeed. . . . But if on her release she be found unclean and polluted by her intercourse with the body . . . it cannot be supposed that she will depart hence pure and uncontaminated. . . . Rather will she become again entangled in that bodily form which, by reason of companionship and intercourse and constant solicitude for the body, has become an essential part of her nature" (*Phaedo*, 81 A.-C.). This passage is imitated by Milton in the Comus, 467 ff.:

> "The soul grows clotted by contagion,
> Imbodies and imbrutes, till she quite lose
> The divine property of her first being;
> Such are those thick and gloomy shadows damp,
> Oft seen in charnel vaults and sepulchres."

NOTE 30, p. 132.

This attack upon the followers of Heraclitus is very appropriately put into the mouth of Theodorus, to whom, as a geometrician, their vague and ambiguous statements must have been peculiarly distasteful. Heraclitus himself derived his title, "the obscure," in great part from the enigmatical brevity of his sentences, but his disciples appear in this respect to have gone beyond their master.

Note 31, p. 134.

In direct opposition to the Heraclitean theory was the doctrine of PARMENIDES that existence is One and unchangeable and eternal, and that change and motion are but appearances. It is in allusion to his words (quoted 180 E.), — "All Being is One and self-contained," — that he is here called "the One." The great chief of the Eleatic school is elsewhere described at the age of sixty-five as "very old and gray-haired, but of noble appearance." — *Parmenides*, 127 B.

MELISSUS of Samos, a statesman and warrior as well as philosopher, was a follower of Parmenides, and a slightly younger contemporary of the Eleatic Zeno.

None of the followers of Parmenides seem to have preserved his doctrines without serious changes. From maintaining all knowledge derived from the senses to be illusory, they finally tended toward complete negation and scepticism.

Note 32, p. 135.

The image suggests that just as the warriors in the Wooden Horse at Troy, although contained in the same image, were complete and independent persons, so our faculties may be distinct entities, not parts of one soul, although contained in the same human form.

Note 33, p. 136.

It has been well remarked, "These ideas must not be measured by their familiarity to ourselves. To the Greek mind they were a revelation and a triumphant vindication of mind over sense." — Jowett.

Note 34, p. 138.

The tablet here spoken of is not a waxen writing-tablet, but a block of wax used for sealing. Locke employs a similar illustration in describing the different kinds of memory.

" If the organs or faculties of perception, like wax overhardened with cold, will not receive the impression, . . . or, like wax oi a temper too soft, will not hold it when well imprinted; or else, supposing the wax of a temper fit, but the seal not applied with sufficient force to make a clear impression, — in any of these cases the print left by the seal will be obscure." — *Human Understanding*, 29, § 3.

NOTE 35, p. 139.

The likeness in Greek between κηρός (wax) and κέαρ (heart) is the occasion of a pun which cannot be rendered in English. The epithet "all-wise poet," which follows in the next speech of Socrates, refers, of course, not to Homer's mistaken praise of the heart's shagginess, but to his knowledge of the human heart itself. — *Il.* 2, 851; 16, 554.

NOTE 36, p. 145.

The duties which devolved upon the ancient kings were afterwards divided between nine archons. One of these officers represented the king in his capacity of high priest, and at the PORCH OF THE KING tried cases of homicide and other acts of impiety. It was here, therefore, that Meletus and Anytus brought their indictment of Socrates.

These porticos or colonnades, of which there were many in Athens, were often attached to temples or public buildings, and formed a convenient protection from the weather, besides being a pleasant lounging-place at all seasons. They were frequently ornamented with paintings commemorating mythical and historical events relating to the history of Athens.

THE END.

www.ingramcontent.com/pod-product-compliance
Lightning Source LLC
Chambersburg PA
CBHW032228230426
43666CB00033B/1641